As I read, I realized that Noelle's story is mine, and likely yours too. It is a story of being ruled by and then letting go of perfectionism. Of trying to numb oneself from facing pain directly. Of somehow finding hope amidst heartbreak. This book is a treasure, and I will cherish it!

> *from the foreword by Anna Whiston-Donaldson,*
> *NYT Bestseller of the book, Rare Bird*

Noelle's *One Slender Thread* is courageous and compelling. She bravely explores deep questions of faith and family, betrayal and redemption, even when she must surrender all that she once held as truth. Noelle honors her life's darkness and light, and all the luscious gray between. Through her fearless seeking, she emboldens us to examine our own hidden depths. Healing waits in these honest, heartfelt pages. Don't miss this one.

> *Amanda Fall, author & creator of The Phoenix Soul*

As a writer and spiritual director, I often use the language of "following the thread" to illustrate our search for the Sacred. Noelle's own search for "one slender thread" and her emphasis on the value of knowing and telling our stories serves as an invitation to dive deep into the waters of the soul where the true self and the Divine can always be found. With her own vivid storytelling, coupled with writing prompts to begin telling your own stories, you'll soon find that when when you follow the thread stitched throughout this moving book your life will never be the same.

> *Lacy Clark Ellman, author of Pilgrim Principles*
> *& creator of A Sacred Journey*

ONE SLENDER THREAD

*Journeying Toward Wholeness, Connection &
Freedom Through the Power of Storytelling*

NOELLE JUDAY

Cover design by Lacy Clark Ellman, www.asacredjourney.net/design/
Cover photo by Nature Art
Title font, Return to Sender, by Tom Kolter

ISBN: 1515361500
ISBN-13: 978-1515361503

To Loryn

Glennon,

Thank you for being one of the first voices to tell me it was not alone; to affirm that I, too, had a story to tell. Thank you for infusing so many of us with courage & hope!

♡ - Noelle Jurday

CONTENTS

FOREWORD

Noelle Juday and I are at different places in life.

I am older than she is, and our children are at different stages. While she is dealing with swim goggles, training wheels and play-doh, my days are more likely to include waiting in a high school parking lot to drive my daughter home, or cruising the mall, well-worn credit card at the ready. I am fairly entrenched in the church of my childhood, whereas Noelle has found herself needing far more mystery and nuance than her conservative Christian upbringing was able to offer her.

Imagine, then, my delight in uttering "me too" from the first page to the last of this beautifully crafted book! With her winsome style, Noelle openly and honestly plumbs the depths of her past, sharing the images, moments, and memories that shaped her into who she is today. Noelle bravely exposes all to the light of examination, choosing what helpful messages to take forward, and what damaging ones to discard.

As I read, I realized that Noelle's story is mine, and likely yours too. It is a story of being ruled by and then letting go of perfectionism. Of trying to numb oneself from facing pain directly. Of somehow finding hope amidst heartbreak.

Throughout the book, Noelle shares words from her favorite authors on each topic she covers. This furthers the idea that we all are more alike than different as we grapple with big ideas such as our purpose, the nature of God, and divine love.

I am often a lazy reader, content to let the author make all the hard choices, while I keep my distance. This is impossible with Noelle's book, for she asks directed, thought-provoking questions ideal for personal reflection and journaling at the end of every chapter. It is not daunting to us, because Noelle models it in every chapter, telling her own story. Not only does she encourage us to write about specific memories from our past, she has us look forward with such questions as, "Where could you use more flexibility in your pursuit of God?" and, "What does the idea, 'things are not what they seem', mean for your life today?" I would have loved simply reading Noelle's wise and transparent story of her life, but having it tied to my own growth added a even more depth and opportunity for application. This book is truly transformative!

Having lost my mother when I was 18 and my son when I was 41, I remember being disabused of my former notion that life is either fair or somehow within my control. I knew I had to try to make sense of my past and find a way to live into a future that was not what I had imagined.

Noelle's book reminded me how writing our lives can help ensure that no experience, no tear, and no struggle is ever wasted.

This book is a treasure, and I will cherish it!

Anna Whiston-Donaldson
Author of *Rare Bird,* a NYT Bestseller

THE END OF THE WORLD

This is the root of the creative work we do: the desire to intimately touch and share the truth of our lives and our world, to find and follow the sometimes-hidden thread stitching ourselves and our reality into wholeness.
Oriah Mountain Dreamer, What We Ache For

The End of the World began in the summer of 2008. It all started when my husband and I made our much anticipated move halfway around the world to Chiang Mai, Thailand. Our goal was to work with a church to start a bilingual school in the city, to get involved in orphan care and to be a part of the modern-day fight against slavery and sex trafficking.

But within weeks of our arrival, we watched as all those years of dreaming and praying and planning began to shatter at our feet. Plans for the school were canceled, and relationship with the church was broken. We soon realized that our reason for being in Thailand was vague, if not altogether lost.

We were foreigners in a foreign land, spinning with culture shock while trying to deal with devastating isolation. Just feeding ourselves often felt like an uphill battle. Reeling with confusion and heartbreak, we found our inboxes full of unnerving news from back home: best friends getting divorced, loved ones falling into addictions, illnesses and financial hardships from every corner of our relational world.

And yet, I would soon discover that the loss and wounding had really just begun. It seemed we had unwittingly boarded a roller coaster of horror, slowly climbing a hill of broken trust, free-falling into spiritual disillusionment, rounding a curve of painfully pat answers, climbing another hill built on spiritual manipulation and shame, plummeting at last with the loss of our first son. For nearly two years, the consistency of bad news became so expected that I dreaded waking up in the morning. I was sad, depressed, suicidal.

In all of this, I felt incapable of voicing my pain, of fully expressing all the raw emotions I was experiencing. I wanted to be that "perfect" Christian I had always strived to be, but I struggled to fit into all the old labels or to apply all the familiar prayers and promises to a life that was no longer recognizable to me. I searched for meaning, for hope, for answers, for just *one slender thread of truth* to make sense of all the mess. But every time, I came up short.

I entered a season of endless crying and questioning. I could not name all that was shifting and breaking inside of me. I grew increasingly frustrated and fatigued from trying to put my heart into words and coming up short and unmet. Finally, on a summer night in 2010, I made a declaration with myself to stop talking about the pain, to stop feeling at all. It was an act of survival and one that I stuck to for the next *three years.*

~:~

I sat up, startled by the unexpected sound of my husband's phone buzzing from the nightstand. Rubbing my eyes and trying to focus in the moonlit room, I watched my husband lift himself to his elbows as he answered the call. His eyebrows creased in concern, and then his face turned white. I could not begin to imagine what the phone call was about.

It was July 6, 2013. We had moved back to the States three years earlier, had our miracle baby, Kyler, and then quickly found out we were pregnant again with our daughter, Havyn. My husband had finished his Master's degree and began his teaching career the year before. I had recently started an online business and transitioned to staying home with the kids full-time. We had learned to live with the pain of our past, or at least to numb and silence the aches and to busy ourselves with life again.

My husband was on summer break and we had just spent a festive fourth of July with my family. Fireworks, cookouts and a slow, lazy afternoon on the porch. We had crashed into bed that night, exhausted from all the sun and play.

When I finally gathered my senses, I realized it was my sister on the other end of the line, urgent in her speech. I listened as she explained that my brother, Jordan, and his girlfriend of five years, Loryn, had been in a terrible car accident. My sister reported a few details of the accident, almost none of which would we remember once hanging up. The only thing that rung abrasively clear, lodged unnaturally in my mind, was this: Jordan was fine, but *Loryn was dead.*

All the family were gathering at the hospital in Logan, and we, too, started to make plans for our trip down. Daniel left immediately with my older sister, and I waited until morning when the kids woke to make the hour trip to my hometown. I drove unsteadily, dreading the reality I would have to face upon arrival.

Bits and pieces of the details surrounding the accident started to come together over the next two days - reports from those that had been at the hospital the night of the accident, hushed conversations from friends and family coming to pay their condolences, newspaper articles and police reports, even the state's morning newscasts. I was desperate for details. Something about receiving one more piece of information gave me a momentary sense of control, helping calm the tide of grief that was swelling inside, even if just for a split-second.

We learned that Jordan and Loryn had been spending the evening at a cookout with her family. Later that night, they loaded up to head home, Loryn in the driver's seat of her red Pontiac Sunfire. As she attempted a left turn onto a curvy country road, they were broadsided by an oncoming minivan. Jordan was able to free himself, but Loryn's side, having received the brunt of the impact, was completely crushed. When rescue workers arrived, Loryn was still conscious and even able to speak. After using the Jaws of Life, she was finally freed and my brother insisted on riding in the ambulance with her, but was denied that privilege. Instead, he met her corpse at the hospital moments later.

What do you do in light of such loss?

I was tormented by the fact that neither Loryn, nor the other driver, was cited for anything that night. There was no rain, no fog, no alcohol or drugs involved. Nobody was speeding or texting or fiddling with their hair. It seemed to be a true instance of being "in the wrong place at the wrong time." A neon sign chiding us, bright and hopeless: *"You don't have a say."*

We mourned as a family all week, awaiting the finality of the funeral. I had only experienced an open-casket funeral once before, eerily enough when my youngest sister's boyfriend was killed in a tragic accident a couple years earlier. I remembered the pale face, the total stillness, the uncomfortable confrontation with my own mortality. But still, I was completely unprepared for seeing Loryn's gorgeous face and petite body motionless in her casket that day. I was overwhelmed with grief, touching her hand, saying goodbye for the last time.

What do you do in light of such loss?

With the funeral behind me, the permanence of Loryn's still, ashen face imprinted on my mind, I felt bewildered and hopeless. Looking back now, it is hard to know whether it was simply the tragedy of losing someone so beautiful and so young, or the fact that Loryn had worked as my assistant all that previous year and I had grown to truly love and respect her, or the reality of watching my twenty-year-old brother navigate the devastation of losing his first and only love - or perhaps, the final straw in the haystack of grief I myself was still carrying at the time, *but I crumbled.*

I have never experienced the unfettered mourning and shattering that I experienced those weeks and months after Loryn's death. Although my mourning could not be compared to her family's, closest friends' and my brother's, it was breathtaking still in its intensity and persistence. I became largely functionless.

More times than I can count, I found myself curled in a corner of the kitchen, sobbing. I would try to connect with the kids, but even tending to their basic needs would seem overwhelming; I would fall on the floor in tears, afraid and hopeless. My mind was consumed with Loryn - all the family events we had shared, all the unspoken words I now carried in deep regret, all the life she would never get to live. My husband would take the kids to the zoo for the day, and I would go for a walk in the woods, lie and cry, sleep.

What do you do in light of such loss?

For the first time in three years, I was forced to face my feelings again. I was forced to acknowledge the pain of loss, the reality of injustice. I let all the old questions rise back to the surface, the deep aches and wonderings and why's. I found myself staring all those stuffed-away emotions from years past in the face, awakened by tragedy and the remembrance of a life gone too soon.

~:~

It was terrifying and overwhelming to feel so deeply again, and yet, oddly exhilarating. I began to read feverishly, as though my life depended on it, as though the words I was reading could somehow sooth the endless aches. And in some ways, they did.

But it was not until I started writing my *own* words that the ache became more bearable. It was not until I allowed myself to revisit my past - unearth all the pain, dig deep into the grief of the present and acknowledge the wounds that still festered - both *in writing and in public,* that something started to shift. It was as if the act of speaking the unspeakable, owning my story, writing out my questions and my fears in all their rawness and mess, somehow began to weave my heart back together. Each word, woven to the next, acted as a stitch in my soul, creating a renewed sense of meaning, perspective, even hope.

I was writing because my soul depended on it, because I needed threading back together. No revisions, just soul-stitching. It is as doctor and author Charles L. Whitfield says, *"The most useful and healing thing about telling our own story is that we, the story teller, get to hear our story. When we tell our story from our hearts, bones and guts, from our Real Self, we discover the truth about ourselves. Doing so is healing."*

That fall, as I wrote, I finally started to find that *one slender thread of truth* that had always alluded me. I started to see with new eyes, to understand and appreciate life in ways I never could before. I dove deep into the feelings of loss and grief that I had run from for over three decades of life and began to rise, to my astonishment, much more alive and breathing full.

I spoke my truth, in many instances, for the first time ever. Hard truths, painful truths, messy truths, boundary-setting truths. I didn't care about all the rules and all the labels and all the masks anymore. I allowed myself to disagree out loud, to voice my questions for all to hear, to speak the unspeakable and to own the deep, even dark, emotions that dwelled within. I gave myself permission to feel true grief and intense joy - often within moments of each other.

And I wrote about it all. I wrote about the mystery and the uncertainty, about waking up and feeling again, about loss and family and finding ourselves. When I shared my stories, I found over and over and over again the powerful craving for courage and authenticity we all have.

~:~

Because of Loryn, I have spent endless hours over the past two years writing my story, looking back through dark corners and long-forgotten details, searching for even *one slender thread* - of truth, of hope, of my true self, of God. And in doing so, I have come upon mercy, unexpected healing and much needed hope. I have witnessed, firsthand, the beauty and the power of finding my voice and telling my story.

Today, I can say that this I know for sure: *You have a story to tell. And so do I.* We each have a story, and as we give voice to those stories - in writing, in conversation, in service - we find the truth of who we are and what this life is all about. We experience the power of storytelling.

Author Sue Monk Kidd captures perfectly the essence of what I have learned about telling our stories when she writes, *"God, the sublime storyteller, calls us into the passion of telling our tale. But creating personal spiritual stories is an act of soul-making that does not happen automatically. It comes only as we risk stepping into the chaos of our lives and naming the angels that inhabit the shadows. It comes as we give expression to our struggle for individual meaning, identity, and truth, as we wrestle with angels, both light and dark, and celebrate the places where God stirs. In the crucible of story we become artists of meaning. There we meet God most surely."*

All my life I have been trying to meet God, trying to make sense of the ache inside me. Today, still, I yearn for the Divine. I yearn for more *connection* with those I love, more *freedom* from all the self-imposed expectations and external demands, more life lived from a *whole heart*. I am a mix of deeply thankful and anxiously unsettled, oscillating between moments of true bliss and satisfaction, and those of endless seeking and striving. I want to grab hold of this life, to make the most of my days. And I want to do it with meaning.

But often, I have gotten lost in my search for meaning. Thinking I have found it, I have hidden for years behind rules, behind religion, behind people-pleasing and perfectionism. I didn't know I was hiding. I couldn't see all the pieces that were broken, all the possibilities that lay dormant in me. I knew there was longing and questions and truth buried deep, but I could not name them *until I started to tell my story.*

Shauna Niequist wrote, *"Every once in a while, when I write, I feel that feeling of a thousand slender threads coming together, strands of who I've been and who I'm becoming..."* I believe when we tell our stories with honest, courageous words, we weave together "a thousand slender threads" from our own lives. We stitch together our days with words, and bring to life new hope and truth, *finding freedom, finding connection, finding ourselves.*

I invite you to tell your story. To visit memories long forgotten and to unearth parts of yourself that have been dormant too long. At the end of every chapter I offer a writing prompt, a chance for you to practice putting your own life into words. Go as deep as you want. Find a friend to go with you. Take a chance, and tell *your* story.

A WINTRY RESILIENCE

If you allow the defrosting process to take place - if you
trust that it will work and choose to endure the
pain - one day you will get your soul back.
Glennon Doyle Melton, *Carry On Warrior*

It's been abnormally cold this winter in Ohio: -5 air temperatures with -20 wind chill factors, or lower. Colder than I have ever experienced in my life, or ever intended to, for that matter. So cold that schools are closing just so kids don't get frostbite while waiting for their buses to arrive (lucky for me, I'm married to a teacher).

Having grown up as a Georgia Peach, I wasn't raised to deal with this much snow and cold. Running outside barefoot all summer with occasional missteps into mounds of biting red ants, fine. Immediately stain treating red-clay-coated play clothes each evening, yep. But life for weeks at a time in subzero weather, *that's* not in my blood.

The only time I remember seeing snow as a child was the Great Blizzard of '92 (not its real name, but how it will forever live in my childhood memories). I remember it so vividly because it happened to come the night of one of my beloved birthday sleepovers. I had a half dozen school and neighborhood girls over for an evening of dancing and sugar and giggles. This was the era of New Kids on the Block, so imagine tween girls with rosy cheeks, wildly flailing around the living room to the beat of "*Step by Step.*" It was fabulous.

Apparently none of the girls' parents believed the weather forecasters (some things never change), who were predicting that several inches of snow would cover our area by noon the next day. And why should they? Not only did they have historical evidence that forecasts can be a tad bit unreliable, there was the equally compelling fact that it was mid-March in Atlanta. Such a quantity of snow seemed impossible.

However, lo and behold, the forecasters were right, and as we drifted to sleep well past midnight, the flurries had already started falling. Sometime well into our slumber, we were startled awake by a gust of wind blowing our front door open. The snow continued to pile up through the morning hours, so that we awoke to a sparkling white lawn.

For us Southerners, it was an astonishing amount of snow. People were largely incapable of navigating the slippery streets and thus, some of the girls and I were happily stranded together late into the afternoon, until their parents were willing or able to traverse the snow-laden roads across town. We layered on whatever cold-weather gear we could find, which wasn't much. In a picture from this day, I'm wearing a sweatshirt with my hands stuffed down into the sleeves for lack of gloves and a pair of canvas Keds slip-ons. Good enough.

We laughed and played and nearly froze to death. As each parent finally arrived, we shared stories of building snowmen and slipping off roads, thankful that nobody had died during their drive over. It was a birthday sleepover for the history books. (And I report all of this as a true Southerner, because, of course, the entire four inches of snow had all melted by the next afternoon.)

~:~

My parents announced that we would be moving back to their childhood hometown in Ohio the fall of my eleventh year. I was slightly skeptical of any of our abilities to survive, given the stories I had heard from cousins about the climate in the North. Still, I was a child that loved a challenge, that embraced new experiences, and I was probably the most eager of all my siblings for this grand adventure north.

We arrived in Ohio in December, and weather-wise, it seemed equal to having plopped ourselves down on an iceberg in the middle of the Arctic Ocean! Within weeks, snow had covered the ground and came and went in droves for *months.* We went for weeks on end without sighting the slightest hint of grass. My childhood had taught me that winter was a season counted by days, but in Ohio, winter is counted in months - *long, cold months.*

Upon our arrival in Ohio, it became obvious we would need to gear up with lots more sweaters and warmer coats, hats, gloves, scarves - things I'd never really owned before. As a tween girl, I had fun picking out all the new gear and imagining my first snowy adventure. I was intrigued by stories of winter excursions and snow days and endless hours of sledding. But all too soon, reality would speak for itself, and I would find myself baffled by the pleasure others found in playing in the snow.

Just the act of getting dressed to go out sledding seemed torture enough for me. First, there was the collecting of at least thirteen pounds of clothes. Then, gathered in the foyer, we began meticulously layering each item onto ourselves, making sure the right seams were tucked into each other just the right way so that no hint of the cold winter air would touch a millimeter of our skin. Socks first, then the leggings (long johns if you were lucky), socks pulled over the leggings, sweatpants, more socks pulled over them, and so on.

By the time all thirteen pounds of clothing were assembled onto your body, you were left with about 70% of your normal range of motion. By then, of course, you were sweating and couldn't wait to go outside and plop yourself down in the first huge pile of snow you found. Which I did, and immediately learned where all my seams had *not* sufficiently met.

Still filled with youthful zeal, I ran and frolicked and tried my hand at a modest sledding hill across the street from our house. But there, too, I was tragically disappointed. The climb up was tedious, given my limited mobility. Once on top, I squirmed and fidgeted, trying to figure out how to bend all those layers adequately enough to squeeze myself onto the tiny saucer that would be my ride back down. Then, gaining speed and losing control, flecks of snow pelted my frozen face until I slammed to a stop in a bank of snow. Stinging and bruised, the ascent began again.

We played for what seemed like hours. Then, not more than eighteen minutes later, I gave up. My hands were red and swollen and no longer had any feeling in them. The cold had reduced my range of motion even further, so that now I was functioning at about 40% capacity. Every step became labored, so that it almost felt like there was some sort of snow gremlin under all that white, pulling at my boots and trying to keep me in place. My cheeks were numb, my face wet with a mix of snow and snot. It was then that I first started to feel a hint of betrayal at all those snowy fairy tales I'd been told.

I headed back inside, and, given that most of my appendages were completely functionless at this point, began what seemed to be an absolutely impossible feat: removing all thirteen pounds of clothing, frozen-stiff and layered with chunks of ice, without the use of my hands. I managed to kick off my boots and rip my icy locks free of my hat. I then somehow shimmied out of the top layer of sweats, writhing like a worm out of moist soil. Since I still couldn't feel my fingers, I was nervous that I would unknowingly crack half the bones in them, like when you munch through your cheek before the Novocain wears off after visiting the dentist. Fortunately, no bones were broken, just the back of a chair that was used for support while getting the second layer of clothing off.

Finally, all layers off, I would learn that this was when the real torture actually began. I ran straight to the bathroom and did what any rational, freezing person would do: took the hottest shower I could. It wasn't until I was totally naked, fully immersed in steaming water and drenched, that I realized a swarm of bees had mysteriously entered the shower with me and were rapidly stinging every inch of my body, focused particularly on destroying my hands and feet, which by now had exploded with this stinging sensation. I thought I was going to die.

Even though I survived, and even though I let my youthful zeal get the better of me with a second snow attempt, I definitely didn't need a third strike to know playing in the snow was not all it was cracked up to be. The hint of betrayal had now turned into full-fledged anger and resentment. I hated snow and continued to despise the cold throughout my teenage years.

~:~

Only recently have I ventured out into the snow again. Building snowmen with my son this winter reminded me of those earliest experiences with the freezing snow - how I hated the cold and vowed in anger never to try sledding again. As I wrote out those memories, weaving sentences out of my experiences, I saw some of Mother Nature's great wisdom emerge. I saw truth come from frozen fingers, reality snap into focus through all that layering and tucking, meaning birthed in snowy second-tries. *And that is the power of storytelling at work.*

Take all that layering for example: When those sock layers, which you thought were so meticulously overlapped, split and leave your ankles immediately frozen from the cold, you realize that sometimes even our *best* efforts to control and protect are not enough. That the chills of life reveal where the seams in our own souls are, easily penetrated and immediately vulnerable to the elements. We realize what it means to be exposed.

For me, this happens very unexpectedly. I'm minding my own business, feeling pretty put together, or at the least, a little less messy. The seams of my heart are all tucked in and tidied up. I'm ready to go out, hopeful even. But then I *go* - to love or to speak my truth or to risk being seen or to say how deeply I care - and suddenly the cold air rushes in through the seams, destroying my sense of security and warmth. A family member gets cancer. A friend has a miscarriage. Plans get canceled. Your kid tells you they don't love you. Or they leave home. Or they don't. And there's always death and heartbreak and adult acne to chill your bones. Then all that tucking and layering, all that loving and hoping, just seems like a waste of time. The seams have split and the cold comes gushing in, unabashed, ready to freeze your very core.

This cycle of freezing has happened to me so many times. I can never seem to get things tucked in and cleaned up enough to keep the winds from penetrating. I try and try to control the elements of life by my furious tucking and tidying, but winds still blow, betrayal still happens, friends still die. And all too soon I find myself standing half naked in the cold. Freezing.

I am caught equally by surprise, weeks or months or years down the road, when I realize just how frozen parts of me have become. I realize I have been walking around, soul-numbed and emotionally clumsy. It doesn't hit me until I desperately need all of me to function at full capacity. It's like the winters of life slowly chill the warmer, more supple parts of me - my creativity, my vulnerability, my voice - until finally, one day, I see I have lost feeling in most of my appendages and I'm only functioning with 40% heart mobility. It's then I see that life has become an exercise of the impossible; like trying to remove all that winter gear with stiff, swollen-cold hands, I fumble through relationships and art and service, just hoping I don't break anything before some feeling returns. Usually nothing breaks, but sometimes it does, *or I do.*

And the defrosting is the most painful part. It stings and you want to run away and never attempt such craziness again. It can hurt to feel, to voice your truth, to love; you'll think, *"God, it was easier to be numb."* And people will resist your change; they'll resist your growing and feeling and becoming your own, and that stings a lot, too. But, as much as I hate it, it seems to be the only way to truly live again. To love again. To get your life back. You have to let your heart defrost, again and again; you have to stand your ground one more day - through all that awful stinging, despite those damn bees - and give life or love or that annoying relationship a crazy, youthful second try.

And then - *this is the real kicker* - all too often the second tries, the valiant attempts to re-engage, to say *"I'm sorry,"* (perhaps for the hundredth time), to pick up the phone, to put down the ice cream, to take a deep breath - these valiant efforts are all too often met with another onslaught of freezing cold air, even colder than the first gust. Trust me, I know from experience. It can feel like just when we've mustered the guts to give it another go, the rug is pulled out from under our feet, and we are left bewildered and angry and screaming into the wind, *"Well screw you, too!!"*

I can't tell you how many times it's felt like that rug has been pulled out from under me - just when I thought I'd found the courage, just when I was sure my heart had finally reached steady ground and was through the painful defrosting stage, just when I knew things couldn't get any worse - *whooosh!* Boom!! There's me, crashing down in a tangle of self-inflicted *"I told you so's!"* and *"What's the point anyway's?!"*

Life can feel so self-defeating on days or months or years like these. It's like the more we engage, the more we put our hearts and our stories and our service out there, the more the cosmos seem to laugh at our efforts and mock our engagement. We start to think it would be so much easier to stay inside ourselves, to remain numb, to conclude it's only the frozen idiots that are enjoying themselves out there. But the truth is, life is *worth* all the messy unlayering and the painful defrosting and even the frozen second tries. I really believe that, especially on the good days.

I believe our souls are worth fighting for, worth sitting through the stings of digging deep. I think this is what Rob Bell had in mind when he talks about the *"hard work of the soul."* He writes:

> It is so hard to look deep inside yourself. My experience has been that very few people do the long, hard work of the soul. Maybe

that's why Jesus said the way is narrow...I'm learning that a lot of people give up. They settle. And they miss out. Anybody can quit. That's easy. I'm learning that very few people actually live from their heart. Very few live connected with their soul. And those few who do the difficult work, who stare their junk in the face, who get counsel, who let Jesus into all of the rooms in their soul that no one ever goes in, they make a difference....they are pursuing wholeness...and it's contagious.

Somehow, against all odds and often against my own will, I find again that life is good. Maybe it's not until the fourth or fifth or sixtieth try at defrosting and engaging, but finally we feel our fingers freely moving over the canvas or our hearts openly loving, and we breathe a deep, warm breath of life. Occasionally, we wake up to the reality that the stinging has stopped completely. That despite the cold out there, all is warm in here.

Because the reality is, life's winters will always come and seek to freeze our cores, and often they will succeed for a season. But in this absurdly short life I have lived, I've seen that the seasons come and go, the snow always melts if we will just let it, and then the warmth of rest and hope and joy will reside in us again. I have seen that even when I've exposed my heart so much that it becomes frozen-stiff from the hurt, slowly, painfully, *surely*, it does defrost and beat again. If I'm even the tiniest bit willing and perhaps a little bit more stubborn, I can make it through the stinging.

And it's all the more likely that I'll come out on the other side if I can hold a hand through the storm. I love what

Anne Lamott says about partnering in our winters in her book, *Stitches*:

> *This is what she had to offer when our dear mutual friend's son grew deathly ill: a promise that we do endure, and that out of the wreckage something surprising will rise. Helen was proof that in the cold wind, if you can lean against others, none of you will blow away. You keep each other from falling or help each other get back up. Someone holds out a hand, or even scared old you may hold out a hand, and a person in need reaches for it and hangs on.*

~:~

Today I find myself with a three-year-old who loves to play in the snow. Sometimes his enthusiasm sucks me in and I cannot help but get excited about the prospect of running and laughing together, albeit in the cold. Now, instead of just thirteen pounds of clothes to collect and meticulously layer, I have a weighty stack for the three-year-old, another for the less-than-willing two-year-old and my own hefty pile. The once tedious preparation process has now been multiplied by three and takes up half of our morning.

And since the kids are *always* at about 70% mobility, as soon as the first layer goes on, they immediately plummet to 40% and quickly lose almost any ability to move at all. They waddle and stumble and usually face-dive into a pile of snow after about the fourth step. We are all instantly covered in snow and snot, and I am especially freezing since I was the last one to get dressed and had to rush the process, missing most seams and usually forgetting my hat and scarf altogether.

But for a minute or two, we are laughing and we are in awe at all that white. We are in love with the beauty around us and we don't notice the cold. We take turns sledding down our little 10 foot hill and we stoop low to explore the mystery below. We notice the icicles forming on the gutters and treat them like nature's ice cream parlor. With our popsicles in hand, we waddle and wander and giggle with every slipper step.

And then we get too cold, almost always in less time than it took us to get ready. So we go inside, dragging slushy snow and leaf bits all over the floor, get undressed, heaping all those layers in a pile for mama to wash later, and finally, curl up with cups of hot milk and a warm blanket on the couch.

Like so much in life, those few moments of adventuring in the snow take A LOT of effort; sometimes, frankly, I'm not up for the challenge. Sometimes I can't bear the thought of all the mopping and laundry and snotty noses. Sometimes it just doesn't seem worth it. *What's the point?!*

But I know the point: that moment of joint laughter as we tumble over in the snow together, that memory of building our first snowman, that meeting of awe and excitement at Mother Nature's offerings to us. Even if just momentarily, I get to experience the goodness of life. I get to laugh and play and love and learn. *I get to live.*

And so I try to breathe those moments deeply and wait patiently through the chills of life, grateful always for the gift of *now*.

Writing Prompt: Explore how the concepts of *being numb* and the *pain of defrosting* apply to your life. In what ways are you, or have you been, numb? What do you use to numb your pain? What would, or did, the defrosting process look like for you?

THE LEAST OF THESE

*If we want greater clarity in our purpose or deeper and
more meaningful spiritual lives, vulnerability is the path.*
Brené Brown, *Daring Greatly*

I have wanted to adopt for as long as I can remember, my
earliest childhood memories forever dappled with this
desire. I can remember at a very young age declaring my
intentions to build my family through adoption. I would
speak with youthful zeal, the injustice of a world with
orphaned children burning powerfully inside of my tiny
body. I grew up appalled by the reality that so many new
children were being brought into the world, when so many
unwanted or untended children were already alive,
unaccounted for. I vowed at an early age never to give birth
myself. Needless to say, I was a bit quirky and very strong-
willed.

I come from a family of five biological children, and had no
direct exposure to adopted children or orphans in those
early years. My first memory of encountering a family with
adopted children was in college, a friend-of-a-friend with
two girls adopted from Russia. With such little outward
input, I can only explain my early and intense passion for
orphans and adoption as a seed planted by God.

In high school, my desire to care for orphans continued to grow, finding fuel in the faces of Indian children. While on a summer mission trip there, we visited several orphanages, holding abandoned babies and singing "Ring-Around-the-Rosy" with deserted toddlers. Although their smiles were bright and contagious, I was heart sick at their parent-less, institutionalized realities. Gray concrete walls and rows of dingy sleeping mats, assembly line mealtimes and infrequent cuddles. I held them close and felt the God-seed within me growing.

After returning from India, I stayed in touch with one of our translators, Sabesh, and began working with him in caring for street children and orphans in his village. I saved and fundraised money to be used in purchasing school uniforms and books for the children, their only chance at breaking the cycle of poverty they were born into. I collected packages of art supplies and toys and books, sending them as Christmas and birthday gifts. Sabesh would faithfully take pictures of the children proudly wearing their new uniforms, excitedly holding up their chosen toy, enthusiastically waving hello to their American "mama."

I worked with Sabesh, sending money and gifts, all through college. Once, the children made cards and Sabesh and his family sacrificially purchased a beautiful sari to send to me for Christmas. I remember opening the package, discovering the beautiful white and gold silk and the piles of paper with stick figures and broken English all over them, and then falling to the ground in humbled, grateful sobs. It was the deep soul gratitude of being true to your heart, living out your passion, and all the fulfillment and joy that follows.

Adoption remained at the forefront of my life mission into early adulthood. So much so, that when my husband first expressed serious interest in marrying me, rather than swooning or kissing, I quickly turned our conversation toward family planning. Not five minutes into our romantic relationship, and I was telling him of my lifelong commitment to never birth my own children, but to adopt several kids instead (at least he knew what he was getting himself into!). It was important to me that he knew the extent of this passion from the get go. It was me *and* adoption, or nothing at all.

And fortunately, he was also passionate about orphan care and open to exclusively building our family through adoption. After a whirlwind courtship and engagement, we got married seven months later, just before my twenty-second birthday. Because neither of us had even graduated college, we expected to wait several years before actually starting the adoption process.

~:~

In the third year of our marriage, Daniel and I moved to Chiang Mai, Thailand. We went with the immediate plan of helping a local church start a bilingual elementary school, but were also drawn to the area because of the great need in orphan care. With multitudes of refugees, child sex trafficking and overflowing orphanages, we were eager to get our hands messy in an effort to fight against these injustices.

Within a few months of moving to Chiang Mai, we had begun filing paperwork for adoption. We soon learned that we should expect a wait of about two years before we would actually be placed with a child, a length of time that seemed both absurd and tragic given the immediate needs we witnessed all around. The fire of justice that had burned within me since childhood could not fathom waiting two more years. I was desperate to start caring for orphans *now*, and that passion soon narrowed to a near-obsession with caring for them in our own home as quickly as possible.

In hindsight, part of the urgency I was experiencing was not solely due to the overwhelming need I saw all around. While that was deeply compelling, we had also recently experienced a devastating betrayal in friendship with the Thai church we had moved to work with and were like fish out of water, floundering around for a reason to be in Thailand at all. Although my husband bravely ventured into new ministry opportunities, I was shell-shocked - deeply hurt, confused, fearful - and could only imagine functioning in a more private ministry. I was also becoming increasingly eager to start a family and flex my identity into that of *mother*.

As fate would have it, around this same time we met a couple of Australian and American families that were involved in the Thai foster care system. The idea quickly took root in my mind as the obvious way to fill our waiting season. Fostering would *finally* allow us to be meaningfully involved in caring for an orphan, and would also satisfy my yearnings for private ministry and steps into parenting. Within weeks, I found myself sitting with an acquaintance at a Thai social worker's desk at the largest government orphanage in Chiang Mai, registering to be a foster parent.

I should have known from that initial meeting what a backwards system we were getting ourselves into. Through my own broken Thai and the translation of the acquaintance that accompanied me, I "registered" to be a foster parent and was told I would be contacted shortly. I do not remember offering much more than my name, address and passport number. I do remember being asked if we had an age or gender preference, and if we would have a place for the baby to sleep. The social worker also wanted to be sure I knew that I could never, ever adopt a child that was in my care through the foster system. For reasons that never could be fully explained, and despite much common sense to the contrary, the adoption system and the fostering system in Thailand are strictly prohibited from crossing paths. *"Not an option!"* she'd said.

But I largely dismissed this harsh warning, unaware of the sort of pending pandemonium it would create in our lives. I was too excited about the reality of holding an orphan in my arms, caring for him or her day in and day out, and too encouraged about how easy the registration process had been. I started busying myself with nursery preparations and began reading mama blogs and parenting books. I passed the time by making hand-painted nursery decorations and meticulously arranging and cleaning every corner of the house. I studied sample schedules for babies and toddlers of all different ages, wrote to mothers I knew asking for advice and anxiously tried to fall asleep, night after night.

Thankfully, our wait was short. Within weeks of my initial interview, and without a home visit or ever having even met Daniel, we were contacted about a baby that would be placed in our care. Initially we were told a four-month-old baby girl would be brought over by the end of the week. Then the following day, true to cultural norms, we were told plans had changed and that we would actually be receiving a seven-month-old baby boy the next day. We ran all over town that evening, purchasing a car seat and clothes for our anticipated arrival.

After a fitful night of sleep, Daniel headed off to work and I anxiously awaited the social worker's arrival. Shortly after lunch, a pickup truck pulled up in front of our home. I can vividly remember the rush of excitement that washed over me, freezing my face into a permanent smile and blurring everything in sight, expect that baby boy.

Two social workers carried a large bag of supplies and a pudgy little boy into our house. They checked out the kitchen, then the bathroom, and finally the bedrooms. They were unsettled at the thought of a baby sleeping in a separate bed, let alone a separate room, from us. I assured them in my sub-standard Thai that separate rooms were very normal in America and that we would move him into our room if he seemed to prefer it.

We sat on the floor in the living room for another fifteen minutes or so; I was trying to get every detail possible about my new charge. Having never needed to converse about babies and formula quantities and nap schedules in Thai, I found myself unable to gather as much information as I felt

I needed. The social workers, on the other hand, did not seem at all concerned about providing me with this information, and were soon passing baby Makham over to me and heading out the door. I stood with him on my hip, silently waving at the screen door as the social workers drove away.

We continued to stand in silence for a moment after the pickup was out of our view, when finally my frozen smile began to descend and I suddenly awoke to the reality of myself and this seven-month-old baby boy, alone in the house. There I was, holding a baby who had been abandoned at birth, found on temple steps in a village at just a few days old. There I was, holding an orphan who had spent the first eight months of his life amongst concrete walls and masses of children. There I was, living my childhood dream, daring to love and nurture this little soul whom others had completely abandoned.

Makham spent most of his first day stony-faced and glassy-eyed, seeming to be as bewildered about what to make of his new situation as I was. Much sooner than I ever could have expected, though, we warmed up to each other and became a natural family. I was "mama," the one that made him giggle, the one that taught him how to use a fork, the one that played and read and sung to him all day long. Daniel, too, was quickly "daddy," cuddling and playing with and protecting Makham as his own.

Perhaps the most stunning, though, were the changes in Makham, as his face literally transformed shapes with each new day of smiles. He began to thrive in our home, hitting all normal developmental milestones right on track, as though he had never spent seven months in an orphanage, as though he had heard and spoken English all his life. He became an exuberant, joyful little guy, his adorable face lighting up any space he crawled into.

Meanwhile, we continued to pursue a separate adoption through the Bangkok office. We made another trip to file paperwork and continued researching agency and funding options. But the more in love we fell with Makham, the more untenable the thought of not trying to adopt *him* became. The more impossible ever living without this little guy, *our* little guy, became.

And so, despite that initial warning, we soon found ourselves walking down every road we could find toward the possibility of making Makham our forever son. Some days hopes were high and the road seemed to be leading us closer to a solution. Other days we were distraught, panicked by the lack of control we had over our own lives. We would find a lead, a friend of a friend with a connection in the Bangkok office, file paperwork and spend hours on the phone, pay fees and then wait. *And wait and wait.* Eventually that lead would fall through, and so we would scramble and start the same process all over again. And again and again, hopes up and hopes down, like a nauseating roller coaster ride.

In all of this, there was a core belief within Daniel and I that God would make a way. Assured by Scripture and friends, we walked with a meek confidence, unable to fathom the Divine not moving on behalf of our little boy, on behalf of caring for orphans and bringing justice to earth. In light of all the hurt and betrayal and trauma we had already experienced since moving to Chiang Mai, Makham seemed to us to be a redemption of sorts. He was a light at the end of a dark tunnel, and as we neared the day that we would move back to the States, the only good we could hold onto from our shortened time of living in Thailand.

And so, we prayed and prayed and prayed, and despite the obvious, tried to believe that God would eventually - *miraculously* - come through. Every day we waited for our miracle. We put our hearts and souls into not just the daily care of our now fourteen-month-old son, but into securing the reality of caring for him forever. We got all the way to just ten days before our departure date, all signs pointing toward a completed adoption. We opened the door to what we thought was a congratulatory, *"Your miracle is finally here!"* announcement, only to hear a soul-crushing, *"No."*

The final word was No.

We were told to deliver Makham to his new foster family the following day for an initial meeting, where we would arrange with the new family a final drop-off date. Too stunned to think, too despairing to even pick myself off the ground, I crumbled into a ball and sobbed. On that hard wooden floor where I had prayed with hope so many times before, where I had played peekaboo with Makham for hours, where I had changed his diapers and watched him learn to crawl and then walk, I melted into a pile of tears.

We endured the next week in an anguished state of wanting to savor every moment together, and also wanting to stop staring our loss in the face every day. Finally the day came to drop Makham off with his new foster family (who were a lovely Australian couple) and say goodbye. I can still vividly picture the new mama holding him as they walked us to our car...hugging us as Makham reached for me to take him and put him in his carseat, as I had done hundred of times before...wrinkling his eyes in a moment of panic as I refused his arms and turned to get into the car without him. And then Daniel and I drove away - in a stunned, scarred silence.

Refusing those out-stretched arms is the most painful thing I have ever done in my life. Not only did the agony of waving goodbye to Makham that day freeze my heart into a state of grief for the next few years, it stole my passion for orphans and adoption. I had put all my hope and heart and effort into caring for Makham, and losing him had sent an arrow into my heart that said, *"It didn't matter. Nothing you do matters."* Despite our courage, despite our love, despite our faith, he was gone. I had dared to "love the least of these," dared greatly, and lost it all.

~:~

For years I could not separate the trauma of having lost Makham from my lifelong desire to care for orphans or to adopt. The two were stuck in a tangled mess, and I silently distanced myself from both. In the midst of that heartache, we decided to try our hand at having biological children, and given our history, that decision was a sort of miracle in and of itself. No sooner had we decided to try this more traditional route, than did we find ourselves in my gynecologist's office looking at an ultrasound of our baby. Our son, Kyler, entered the world just over a year after we had waved that final, heart-wrenching goodbye to Makham.

Kyler was a difficult newborn, and in the wake of sleepless nights and hours-on-end of unexplainable crying, we found out I was pregnant *again*. Honestly, the news was devastating at first. The thought of a second baby to nurture and teach and raise was overwhelming, from a spiritual perspective more than anything. My faith was still shattered from our Thailand losses and I was struggling just to keep up with Kyler's immediate needs.

After an extremely difficult first trimester, I started to rest into the reality of welcoming a second child. And as my pregnancy progressed, so too did my excitement and joy. Two weeks before Kyler's first birthday, we welcomed his baby sister, Havyn, into the world. She was a sweet, easy baby - the perfect anecdote to her brother - and soon stole our hearts.

In many ways, our family felt complete. Except, when on occasion, the topic of adoption would resurface. At first I would dismiss the idea completely, dumbstruck by my husband's continued interest in something so risky and painful. Finally, I allowed myself to embrace the concept of adoption from a distance, but could not bring myself to think of adopting as an imminent event in our lives. Instead, we began speaking of adoption as something we would do once our own children were older. My heart needed more time to heal, and plus, I argued, *wouldn't it be better for the kids to be more mentally and emotionally involved in the decision?* I rationalized my own fears with this delay-tactic, and that reasoning worked for a year or so.

But then, as my soul began to defrost from the numbness of pain and grief - both from the loss of Makham and from the tragic death of my brother's girlfriend - my heart began to soften to the natural passions still alive and well within me. For the first time in years, I found myself thinking of adoption with joy, and even longing. I did not want to waste another day denying the good work of adoption that had been planted in me since birth. I realized that, even though my passion for adoption and caring for orphans had been stolen for a season, I could choose to take it back. I could choose to own this God-seed and walk in it again, despite the pain, despite the loss, despite the continued uncertainty of life. I could dare again, and as Theodore Roosevelt put it years ago, *"if he fails, at least {he} fails while daring greatly."*

Writing Prompt: Write about a time you *dared greatly.* What did that daring feel like? How has the success or failure of that daring continued to shape your life?

SPAGHETTI ORPHANS

It takes uncommon humility to carry the dark side of things.
It takes a kind of courage to carry the good side, too.
Richard Rohr, *Everything Belongs*

We were having dinner the other night, my two-year-old daughter, three-year-old son, the hubby and I. Mealtimes at our house are amongst the most chaotic and stressful moments of our days. They're nothing like the movies, where children sit quietly and mom and dad converse about their day while passing around steaming bowls of home-cooked yummies. No, at our house the children are akin to untamed beasts, the food is in various degrees of preparedness and conversation is light and sporadic, usually focused on directing the children in what seem like obvious behaviors even for a two and three-year-old: "P*lease don't put your hands in your spaghetti*," "*Hey buddy, don't rub your messy hands all over your hair*," "*Ahh, No! Don't touch me with those hands!*"

It's been our goal and practice since the kids were born to sit down to a meal together every evening, and yet it is a rare millisecond in time that all four of our rears are actually seated at the table at once. We always forget the napkins or the drinks or the toast still in the toaster, or the fact that one couldn't possibly eat broccoli with a BLUE fork. Just when we think we're finally ready, the chaos reaches a whole new dimension. One child drops a fork, then the other child insists on being able to help retrieve said fork. In their generous but rambunctious attempts to help, second child spills an entire plate of food, while first child tips over her cup. Now we are all back out of our seats, on our hands and knees, picking up hot noodles, wiping up puddles of water and at least one of us is in tears. Nobody has taken a bite of dinner.

Yes, this exact thing just happened.

So, the other night when we found ourselves all simultaneously seated and there was an actual moment of silence, my son asked, "*What do you want to talk about?*" This is my favorite line during any such millisecond of quietness and I was impressed by his awareness that we were, in fact, within such a rare moment. I had plenty swelling in my heart to talk about, so I jumped at the opportunity and said, "*Do you guys think we should start taking care of babies that don't have mama's?*" My husband gave me a wry glance that could have either meant, "*Good luck conducting this conversation in the three seconds you'll have between flying spaghetti!*" or "*Hmmm, what's going on in that head of yours?*"

I continued, "*Mama's been thinking a lot about something, and I want your opinions. What would you do if you were a baby without a mama?*"

Now, if you are even an ounce as judgmental or questioning as I can be, you're probably thinking, "*That's an awfully brash introduction into a heavy dinnertime topic,*" or perhaps, "*That doesn't seem like an appropriate conversation for a two and three-year-old to be having*" or maybe even, "*Why wouldn't you just ask them about their day, lady!"* To which, I would probably offer a sweet smile, then shrug as I inwardly ridicule myself for my ineptness at being a mother.

Or, if I were feeling braver and being truer to myself, I would answer that at heart I am a seeker, a thinker, a melancholic. I often live in a place of *"What's our purpose?"* and *"How can we make meaning out of this moment?"* There are many times that I'd love for the chaos of the day to override the demanding internal drives toward a bigger picture, but it just never seems to happen. And caring for orphans had been weighing heavily on my heart lately, so I was eager to speak to my family about it.

I would also say, that although the language changes a bit, I believe strongly in honoring my children's humanity and intelligence by bringing them into most of my conversations. Obviously there are times when the topic is just not age appropriate, but I believe those instances are much rarer than many others believe. "Adoption," "orphans" and "death" are vocabulary words my children are aware of and have personally experienced in some capacity. I'm a firm believer in the practice of open dialogue.

Back at the dinner table, my three-year-old son, Kyler, replied, *"I would run and run and say, 'I want my moooommy.'"* I responded, *"Yeah, if you didn't have a mommy you would probably feel really sad and lost, huh?"* My daughter, Havyn, sat opposite me nodding her head affirmatively and crinkling her brow at the sadness of such a thought. She is already quite the little mama herself, dressing and undressing her baby dolls, pushing them around in strollers and shushing them on her lap all day long. She was clearly distressed by this image, as was I. *"So, what should we do?"* I pushed, realizing that it had now been nearly ten seconds since anyone got out of their seats. Kyler answered, *"Say, 'Come here, baby, come here, sshh, sshh, sshh.'"* Both kids started to pretend they were cradling a baby and shushing it comfortingly in their arms.

My soul stood in awe and breathed deeply at their courageous, yet simple, responses.

Of course, the moment was quickly lost, because the next thing I knew Kyler's baby had turned into an airplane and was flying around his head, diving into his plate of food and emerging as even messier, mostly red hands. Havyn quickly followed suit and our millisecond of calm vanished as effortlessly as it had appeared. The next ten minutes were filled with more flying noodles, more obvious admonitions and perhaps a few more gray hairs.

Later on, I thought about how lovely it was to hear my son mimic me with his, *"What should we talk about?"* and how beautiful the kids' responses to my questions were. I thought about how sincerely we mean something and how quickly we get distracted away from it. I thought about all the times I felt so compelled toward some good, so sure it was the only way I could take another breath, and yet days, months, years later, I still had not acted. I thought about what a waste of energy good intentions are.

Then I thought about the image my son created of babies running and running and crying, *"I want my mooommy"* and how very simple and yet extraordinarily difficult it would be to scoop one or two of them up and shush them for a moment, or a lifetime. I thought about purpose and meaning and what it would look like to stop getting so distracted. To just do what our hearts say. I thought about all the times I attempted to do just that and felt so painfully thwarted in my mission. I thought about how easy it is to give up, and what it would look like to try again, despite it all.

~:~

Prior to moving to Thailand, Daniel and I had both been heavily involved in, what I would now call a conservative, fundamentalist line of Christianity. I always felt there were a million specific rules I needed to follow and lots of expectations I had to live up to. There was a right and a wrong answer to every possible human question. As a people pleaser by nature, this kind of Christianity quickly defined my world and took over my heart. As a result, I didn't listen to secular music, I felt watching TV was a sinful waste of time, I wouldn't shop on Sundays, I judged anyone who took even a sip of alcohol and I attended *every. single. meeting.* I only knew blacks and whites. If a rule was a rule, I aimed to keep it to the Nth degree.

In many ways, my husband and I were model Christians in our little circle. We lead groups, organized retreats, worked on staff at our church, and sold everything we owned to move overseas as missionaries when we were in our early twenties. Leading up to our move, we tried to do *everything by the book*. We prayed, we fasted, we waited for elders to say *"Ok,"* we matched our skills and dreams with the needs on the mission field, we visited, we planned, *we really believed we were called to go*. And then we went.

{Anytime I write about my previous religious experiences, I always feel a need to offer lots of exceptions and apologies. There are at least three reasons I feel so compelled to do this. One, because I still have a few very dear, very intimate friendships from those years and those circles. Two, because there was life and truth even in the midst of all the rules and confusion. And three, because I am so utterly aware that I don't have all the answers now, either, and can only attempt to speak in truth and love about where I am and what I see at this stage of my journey.}

It was a confusing and crushing reality check when all those years of *doing everything right* fell in a heap at our feet within weeks of moving to Thailand. The church we'd spent years building a relationship with and planning to work with reneged their end of the offer - *eight weeks after* we arrived. This was especially painful for me, as almost a decade of my life had been spent in relationship with this church and so much of my faith journey was wrapped up in them. It was hard to distinguish truth from the mess of our present situation.

But we stuck it out, devoting ourselves to the language and turning to what we knew: fasting, prayer and our church leaders' advice from back home. Within six months of moving, we were very capable in spoken Thai and had learned to read and write at a basic level. Daniel had found a new school to work with full-time and I'd refocused my energies on caring for our foster son. Spiritually and emotionally, however, we were depleted and depressed.

Over the course of the next year, I felt like I was living one of those nightmares where no matter how much energy you exert, no matter how hard you try, you cannot get your legs to move fast enough to carry you away from the bad guys. And there seemed to be a lot of bad guys in Thailand. We kept running and running and hoping and trying and praying we would wake up from the nightmare soon. I thought, *As soon as we wake up, it'll all be okay. God will be there and He'll make sense again - life will make sense again.*

Instead, we found ourselves in the wake of more broken relationships, more betrayal, more shattered dreams. Having our foster son of six months taken away was the final straw. I felt I had been hit with a sledge hammer over and over again, and I could not begin to understand how all of this was happening to me - *God, I followed all the rules; I did it by the books, by Your Book. Why is all this happening? And where are You??* Nothing in my previous belief structure equipped me to handle all the loss and pain and emptiness we now faced. I was angry, hurt and confused - I had known promises that lead to happiness, or suffering for Christ, but not tragedy for no reason at all.

Even after we returned to the States, there were a million things that added to our hurt and anger. There was God, who seemed to have gone on vacation and had no plans of returning anytime soon. Then there were all those well-meaning people who said really, really stupid, hurtful things. And then there were former friends who were unequipped to handle the mess of us in our tragedy, making us feel like we couldn't count on anyone. I soon found myself suicidal, ready for a divorce and desperate to be a mama again. *Life was a total disaster.*

In my desperation to live again, I consciously started numbing the pain and forgetting anything that had to do with Thailand. I was furious with my tears and stuffed them down, down, down. I told the skies, *"You won't hurt me anymore!"* I refused to speak Thai with my husband and had an immediate bias against anyone that appeared even half Asian. I couldn't bear the thought of adoption anymore, so I took life into my own hands, deciding to try to get pregnant. We stopped attending church and I rarely talked to God. As Glennon Melton Doyle put it, *"I prayed in the only way I know how to pray - in moans and accusations and apologies and tears and wild promises."*

In hindsight, I did everything I could do to erase the past in the hopes that I'd erase some pain along with it. Which, as could easily be assumed, did not quite work. But life did settle down, and it did get a little easier: we bought our own home, decorated two nurseries, stabilized in our jobs and welcomed two beautiful, strong, healthy babies into the world.

And yet, it was well past the three year anniversary of our move back from Thailand before I finally realized just how *good* our lives really were. Honestly, I had gotten so used to being a victim and feeling like crap that I had not been able to, or willing to, recognize the goodness and call it *good.* I held a heavy grudge and had grown quite comfortable with the weight of that load. It felt awkward to walk without it. Part of me didn't want to move on.

It was as if putting the load down somehow communicated that I was accepting all the loss and betrayal, that I was saying having our foster son taken away was okay. I felt I had to keep carrying that grief, keep showing the wounds to others, to justify the pain and declare the injustice. I was afraid of forgetting, and scared of becoming that "Follow the Rules" girl again. I didn't want to go back, but was unable to move forward. And so for years, my heart stood still.

~:~

As I write today, it has been almost a year since I started owning *goodness*. It's been a slow process, with the natural ebbs and flows of the soul. Some days I embrace *good* much more willingly than others. On my most courageous days, I let myself look around and *smile*. I let myself laugh and dream and plan for the future. I let myself feel joy and love and hope and intimacy and peace. I let myself *feel*. I remember what Anne Lamott says, "*Your problem is how you are going to spend this one odd and precious life you have been issued. Whether you are going to live it trying to look good and creating the illusion that you have power over people and circumstances, or whether you are going to taste it, enjoy it, and find out the truth about who you are.*"

Today I know, I get to choose being true to my dreams and celebrating the good. I get to choose owning my story and voicing the questions. I get to choose what to do with the gift of this life.

Writing Prompt: Write about the most courageous thing you have ever done - why it took so much courage, how you mustered that courage, and what the outcome was.

FINDING MY FEET

*Hope is definitely not the same things as optimism. It is not the
conviction that something will turn out well, but the certainty
that something makes sense, regardless of how it turns out.*
Paul Rogat Loeb, *The Impossible Will Take a Little While*

In January of 2014, a couple months before Havyn and
Kyler's second and third birthdays, we started researching
adoption again. We weighed the pros and cons of adopting
internationally versus domestically, investigated the foster
care system and foster-to-adopt programs, scoured the
internet for an agency that seemed to be a good match for
our family. We researched and made lists, deciding on one
route one week and then, after more thought and research,
switching to another route the next.

Then, just days after the kids' birthdays in March, we
agreed on international adoption and chose our agency. We
filed a pre-application online and were filling out our
official application paperwork within a week. By April
2014, we submitted our first payment and officially began
the adoption process again.

As a part of our initial adoption application, we had to
specify which country we wanted to adopt from. Daniel and
I were both certain Africa was the right fit, but within that

continent, our agency had several programs to choose from. We read up on each, weighing the pros and cons of all, knowing that uncertainty is an absolute certainty in the adoption world. Finally, we chose the Democratic Republic of Congo, mostly because on paper it seemed logistically easiest - necessitating the shortest travel and having the youngest children available within the quickest time-frame. (Spoiler Alert: none of these are actually true.)

Initially my desire was to adopt a newborn, which by and large is not an option internationally. I knew from our own experience with foster care what a difference in-home parental care can make in a child's earliest months, which is why Daniel and I had originally wrestled over whether or not to go through the foster care system again, instead of trying an international adoption. I knew, too, that even if a child is matched as a newborn internationally, often the court proceedings and immigration processing take long enough that the child is a year or two old once finally brought home. I struggled emotionally at the reality of our future son or daughter having to live his or her earliest, most vulnerable days without us.

I was still grieving the thought of not getting to care for our baby from birth when we attended an adoption training at our agency's headquarters. During the training, we got to meet other adoptive families and hear their stories, some of whom had already adopted one or more children. We got to see photos of orphanages and children in the DRC and browsed the "Wall of Dreams" with photos of children who had been matched to waiting families. It was the first time in my life I had been surrounded by a room full of people with the same deep yearning to care for orphans that I had grown up knowing. I was moved, both by the families daring with us, and by the need of the countries our agency worked with.

By the time we left training that day, my grief had been overcome by the vision of something greater, something so much bigger. We eagerly altered our home study to specify a willingness to adopt a sibling group, with children up to age five. We were open, impassioned, available. And now it was time to get down to the reality of completing our home study.

For anyone who has adopted or gone through the home study process, you know that the first few months of an adoption journey entail an endless list of paperwork that need gathered from any and every official building throughout the city. Local police records, fire inspections, finger-printing, medical checks, FBI background checks, birth certificates, marriage certificates, tax records, bank records, state police clearances, employee verification letters, and on and on. Every item has to be notarized and some have to be apostilled, which basically means verifying the notary's notary. It is a series of safe-guards intended to protect these vulnerable children - and also extremely tedious. We rushed through collecting all of our paperwork, not wanting any part of the process within our control to take a day longer than necessary.

By late Spring, just a couple months after our initial application, we were mailing in our final items and having our last home study interview. And then, before the final draft of our home study had even been approved, before we could catch our breath from all the finger-printing and notarizing and running here and there, we got a phone call with a referral. A six week old baby boy (I'll call him Baby E) was available to be matched with a family, and our agency was ready to pass the referral on to us.

We had not expected to receive a match so quickly, certainly not of a child so young. Just a few months earlier, I was only beginning to consider adoption as a distant possibility, and just a year before that, I was closed to adoption completely. The process of opening my heart to adoption again had been both exhilarating and terrifying. I had denied this passion for so long. Yet, here we were, standing in a park while our kids played, giggling with friends over pictures of a tiny six week old Congolese boy that could one day be *our son*. It was almost more than my heart could bear.

Official referral paperwork was sent later that week, including medical reports and a history of Baby E's life. The brief biography stated that Baby E had been found by a river by a "nice, old woman" and brought to a local orphanage when he was just a few days old. The medical reports estimated his birthday as April 30, and cleared him of a few major medical issues. But a majority of the medical paperwork was blank, and we soon learned that all referral paperwork is potentially fraudulent or incomplete and therefore should be taken as such. If we agreed to a referral, it would be with the understanding that, essentially, we knew nothing more about the child than what one blurry face shot told us.

Our agency gave us a week to decide whether or not to accept this referral. During that week, the U.S. State Department held a conference call with all adoptive or prospective adoptive parents trying to adopt from the DRC. The call was in response to a visa ban that had been put into place by the Congolese government the previous Fall (sadly, still in place at the time of publishing). Since the ban began being enforced, hundreds more adoptions had been finalized by the Congolese court systems and hundreds more families had begun the adoption process. Not only that, but hundreds of families had found themselves in limbo, with completed adoptions but no way to get their children out of the country.

Daniel and I had been aware of a visa ban in the DRC, but were not aware of the reach of its effects or what was happening in the meantime. We had considered it *"one-of-those-adoption-world-things,"* having been well-acquainted ourselves with the unnerving twists and turns of international adoptions. We assumed if the country was still processing adoptions, and if the agency was still soliciting applications, the problem would work itself out sooner rather than later.

The tone of the conference call, however, was much bleaker. We quickly became aware of the gravity of the situation, learning the numbers of families with children who had been in waiting for years because of the ban. We heard complaints about the lack of progress and cooperation on the Congolese government's side, as well as the lack of urgency and initiative on the American government's side. We heard from ambassadors and representatives of the Secretary of State, as well as from families who knew both systems inside and out from having lived this nightmare over the past year.

Toward the end of the call, a prospective adoptive parent finally spoke up and asked, *"What sort of effect will this ban have on new families entering the adoption process in DRC?"* The main speaker gave her usual diplomatic response, but then broke character and said, *"If you want my honest opinion, ma'am, you should really find another country!"* For a moment I couldn't breathe. I hung up from the call, deflated and confused.

How could we accept a referral of a child that may never make it to our home? How could we knowingly start walking down such a treacherous road of high hopes and deflated dreams? We knew better! Hadn't we been here, done that?! Wouldn't it be wrong to put our kids through the ups and downs, to put ourselves through all that heartache again?

I was depressed the rest of the day, and convinced that there was no way we could move ahead with the adoption of Baby E. All the old fears and traumatic memories started replaying through my mind. Of phone call after phone call - *good news, bad news, good news, bad news* - of cumbersome bureaucracies and uncontrollable outcomes, of expectant prayers and final *"No's."* When Daniel and I finally got a chance to speak about the situation post-bedtime, I expressed my growing hesitations.

But Daniel had processed the phone call very differently. He, too, was disappointed and concerned, but the news didn't shake him the way it had shaken me. He already felt a connection, even an obligation, to Baby E, and was willing to walk this road wherever it took us. I struggled to understand his quick connection, having proceeded with such emotional caution myself, and realized the only obligation I had felt was to our kids and protecting my own heart.

We talked well into the night, wrestling through our emotions, the fate of this baby boy we hardly knew and the reality of the current political situation. Our choices were ultimately to accept Baby E's referral, or to switch countries completely. We were at a place in our adoption process where such a switch would mean little extra paperwork and no extra money. But just one more day, just one quick *"yes,"* and we would have tens of thousands of dollars invested into DRC. And hearts tied to a specific little baby, waiting for us.

~:~

We validated the fears and honored the caution. We considered our children, their hearts and their futures, their routines and their expectations. We considered our own hearts and spoke of the pain, the memories, the reasonable hesitation we felt to walk down this uncertain road. We respected the Secretary of State's opinion and knew that we would not be wrong to switch countries, that perhaps switching would be the most sane thing to do. We honored reason and our freedom to choose.

And, ultimately, we chose Baby E. More broadly, we chose DRC. We chose to commit to a country whose history of war and famine and brutality is truly incomprehensible. We chose to be a part of a program investing in the lives of orphans where few else are - where processes are just developing, where corruption is common, where hope is sparse. We chose to accept Baby E's referral, no matter the wait, no matter the outcome, as an answer to our passion to care for orphans *today*.

Writing Prompt: What is the hardest decision you have ever had to make? What factors weighed into the decision? How did you decide which road to take, and have you been satisfied with your decision?

MYSTERY

*If my religion is true, it will stand up to all my
questioning; there is no need to fear.*
Madeleine L'Engle, *Walking on Water*

The idea of living a hopeful, happy life in the midst of uncertainty has been revolutionary for me. And after spending the last few years reeling from loss, wallowing in a lot of anger and resentment, and doing my best to simply numb all the pain and uncertainty away, a revolution is exactly what I needed.

Occasionally I'd find myself speaking openly about all the hurt and questioning, and trying to process myself to a place of peace. But in reality, I hated where my life was. I hated having been knocked off my comfortable horse named "This is the Way." I hated facing the reality of just how out of control we all really are - regardless of what we think we know or who told us we should know it. I hated facing life outside of my religious bubble and frankly, was completely unprepared to do so.

Because the truth is, vulnerability can hurt and uncertainty is extremely uncomfortable. I am learning just how hard it is hard to live in the gray, to embrace the mystery, to *be* the questions - it feels so wishy-washy, like I am walking in sand in a pair of new stilettos. I'm never exactly sure what the next step will bring: *firm footing or sinking insecurity.* Usually, it's a bit of both.

Although I have grown increasingly confident that my spirit soars in the freedom of uncertainty, that there is life within the unanswerable and that true spirituality is intimately paired with questions and searching, these truths did not come to me easily. I am well acquainted with the discomfort that so much gray brings, and the theological and practical dilemmas that so much unknowing evokes. With each breath of hope, I sense a suffocating blow of hopelessness just around the corner. *Can this really be done? Can I flourish in the mystery that is life? How do soul and uncertainty abide together?*

~:~

I purposely shut down a lot over the years, told myself not to feel and not to engage. I invested everything in my kids. There was some lingering hope that *things would get better,* but I had no words for what that meant or how that might happen. I mostly numbed and looked the other way, unaware that there is much life to be lived *in* the questions and *in* the pain. I managed to avoid the reality that another blow could come again - would, surely, come again. That loss is always a part of life. I lived aloof and mostly detached.

Then, my family experienced that unthinkable tragedy: two high school sweethearts, separated in a deadly car accident. It was one of those phone calls that momentarily lifts you out of your seat and catapults you into an out-of-body existence as you try to grasp at what was just said and place it within real life. What? How? *Why??* When my feet landed again, I found the sickening reality of a life cut far too short, a love ripped away and an entire community in utter dismay.

But, oddly enough, I also found my soul. I saw my brother shattered beyond imagination and finally realized, *"This is life. Pain and loss, nobody is immune."* I stepped outside of my numbing, my "victim shell" and finally allowed myself to grieve - for my brother, for Loryn's family, for Loryn, and for all the other losses I had avoided over the years. I had to reckon with the reality that I was still alive, that I'd been given a gift of breath today and was responsible for what I did with it. I had to own that life doesn't stop just because I check out. *I had to check back in.*

Part of checking back in for me meant re-engaging my soul with the world, and I did that largely through reading and writing. Honestly, at the time, I hadn't read a book for at least three years and had perhaps never read literature truly of my own choosing. But when I finally picked up a book, it was like my soul was famished from the fast and I just couldn't get enough. I read and read and read and read. My precious husband, who was on summer break at the time, allowed me space to indulge that appetite. So I did; I ate up book after book.

In my binge, I repeatedly came across authors who seemed to have similar messages to share, messages that I never, ever remember having heard before. There were so many words that gave me hope, that continue to stir my soul awake today. They were treasures to me in my mourning and wandering, and are treasures to me still in my living.

I'd require you to read a stack of those books right now if I could and then invite you over for a cup of coffee and a long chat about what all the words in them mean to you. They have meant life for me. Like this quote from Rob Bell: *"A Christian doesn't avoid the questions; a Christian embraces them. In fact, to truly pursue the living God, we have to see the* **need** *for questions. Questions are not scary. What is scary is when people don't have any. What is tragic is faith that has no room for them."*

Oh, if I had heard those words a decade earlier! If I had had the space in my soul to receive them so much sooner, I would have spared myself years of angst and guilt and confusion. I would have spared others my religious fundamentalism and my quest for absolute perfection. I would have been able to see that the questions I was always battling to silence were perfectly welcome, and were not the enemy.

And if I had heard these voices sooner, I would have known I wasn't alone. I would have found companionship and belonging and unexpected hope from those brave souls willing to share the truth and messiness of their journeys, like these words from Sue Monk Kidd from her book, *When the Heart Waits:*

> *"If I can't trust God now, when I need him most, how can I ever trust him again?" she cried. She didn't understand that there was a journey to be made here. A waiting, a gestating, a slow and uncertain birthing. That is where God was to be found. Not in the erasing of the experience, but in the embracing of it...Most of us*

Christians don't know how to wait in pain - at least not in the contemplative, creative way that opens us to newness and growth. How did we ever get the idea that God would supply us on demand with quick fixes, that God is merely a rescuer and not a midwife?

I cannot express in words what authors like these did for me, for my soul. I felt like I was reading *hope* penned. Like I could finally breathe again. Like I was right where I was meant to be.

For the first time that I could ever remember, I felt safe in my unknowings, even esteemed in my questioning. I felt an immense freedom to embrace my journey, my truth, my life. I felt liberated to be me, completely undefined and unedited. Finally I could see that the gray I had found myself in for years wasn't detestable mirky waters, but rather possibility-infused springs. If only I would accept the mystery, embrace the gray, true life awaited.

~:~

It's been months since I first stumbled across those life-changing authors and their morsels of wisdom. Their messages to me continue to resonate and define much of my journey.

Be the mystery.
Live the questions.
Know you don't know and know that's okay.
But hope.
Love.
Live your life.

It's harder than it sounds, really. I get it wrong most days. I sense my pursuit of life in the gray rubbing against two extremes. On the one side, there's the put-together, deeply religious, the Bible-*is*-the-answer voice that's apprehensive about the relativistic nature of so many *"Maybe's"* and *"Well, we don't really know's."* I feel backed against a wall, required to choose and define life neatly into labeled boxes, black and whites, wrong and rights. Sometimes I find myself longing for the simplicity of such labels again, drawn to the ease of certainty. I fear not being able to see past the curve in the road ahead and wonder how far I can go with so much undefined.

But on the other side, there's a gruffer voice, a voice worn from wondering and wailing out loud. A voice that recoils at religious language, that resists the answers, that shrugs off any claim of knowing as ignorance or arrogance. It draws me into a different sort of dogma, a staunch stance of Maybe. It refuses knowing and clings to the questions. It tells me religion could never be, God could never be, perhaps, even, good could never be. It pulls me into despair, tells me there's no point anyway, just do what you want. One extreme retaliating with another extreme.

Both voices call out to me and I teeter-totter slightly, up and down, up and down, trying to understand, to see where each road leads. I read ravenously and I write, seeking desperately to weave myself into the middle, to bury my roots away from either extreme. *I long for truth more than answers, wholeness more than comfort.*

Ultimately, this has become my aim: *To breathe in the hope of faith and breathe out the calm of mystery.* To embrace the discomfort inherent in both faith and mystery. To welcome the truth and the questions. The knowing and the unknowing. To learn to live balanced, in the middle, in the mystery that is life.

Writing Prompt: How does the reality of *mystery* fit into your life? Write about a time you were uncertain and how you handled that unknowing.

TEARS

*Story allows me to enter the tension between memory and hope. When
we enter our personal story, we embark on an odyssey of reconciliation,
of reclaiming more of who we truly are, the selves that are
dark and light, redeemed and unredeemed.*
Sue Monk Kidd, *Firstlight*

Memories intrigue me more and more these days - how
completely objective and grounded in reality they are, and
yet, too, how deeply subjective and relative in nature they
are. If you think about memories as one soul's perception of
an experience, one mind's reaction to a word or a touch or
a taste, you soon realize that memories are as numerous
and varying as individual souls themselves. Not at all that
memories are fictitious, and certainly not irrelevant, but
incomplete on their own. I have learned with new respect
to hold my memories out, turning them over and over,
looking at them from every angle and yet holding closely
the reality that even in all I see, there is still more to the
story.

As I rely on my memories to write, I am confronted
constantly with the reality that what I recall in every event
of life is truly a personal possession. My memories are just
that - *mine*. They are pieces of me, layered one upon
another, filtered through all the personality and
experiences and values that make up me. Writing about my

life - my childhood and my faith and my marriage - is a wide-open act. Both because I am baring my own soul on paper, and because the reality that I represent in my writing may come into conflict with the reality that others remember. I think every couple can relate to this phenomena, when one spouse recalls a conversation with certain words and tones and actions, and the other spouse recalls a very different set of words and tones and actions. Whether we intend to be or admit to be, we are all biased, and thus, too, are our memories.

When I write, I often find that my memory of an event, a person or a place is initially very flat. It takes time and space to work up a fuller recollection in my mind, to draw back into the present what is somewhere tucked away in my subconscious. I have to sit with a memory for a few days or even weeks, letting new details rise to the surface. Even then, there are often holes; even then, I am deeply aware of what a personal treasure each memory is.

For me, the value of memory recollection, like the value of writing, is to find understanding and a deeper sense of who I am and what I am here for. As I weave together pieces of my life and fragments of myself, I see a bigger picture and a deeper meaning. I get to hold pieces of my childhood again, penned in black and white, and learn about the child I was and the world that shaped me. I get to freeze time with each sentence, bringing the past and the present and the future into one written space. I get to walk away with new understandings of a person or an experience, which inevitably leads me to greater love and empathy for them, and for myself.

And so I have ventured into my own abyss of memories, stirring up the dark depths to see what I will find. Letting one memory at a time rise, often writing about that recollection until I have filled in every gap I am capable of pulling into my consciousness. Sometimes it is long and tedious and feels unfortunately fruitless. Sometimes, despite the time and effort, it is magical and meaningful and deeply freeing.

~:~

The first time I ever remember seeing my parents hug was when my mother's father passed away from cancer in 1992. I would have been nine at the time, and my mother would have been entering her third trimester of pregnancy with her fifth and last child, my baby brother. My mother received a phone call with the news of her father's passing in our kitchen. I remember the light oak cabinets behind her, the speckled tan countertops she leaned against and the oatmeal linoleum underfoot. I remember the long phone cord twisting back into a tight knot when she hung up the phone and the tiny click from the receiver when she put the phone gently back in its place.

I'm not sure if my dad was in the room during the phone call or not, but he must have entered shortly after either way, because the next thing I remember seeing is my parents locked in each other's arms. I have a crystal clear picture of my dad's dark, wavy hair, his suntanned neck, his strong, wide back, calmly and completely covering my mother. I only knew my mom was behind him because of the sound. This was also the first time I ever remember seeing or hearing my mother cry.

My Pop's funeral was scheduled later that week, back in my parents' hometown of Logan, Ohio. I do not have memories of having traveled there prior to this funeral, even though we had a myriad of aunts, uncles, cousins, great aunts, great uncles and second cousins in the area. And I have very fuzzy, childlike memories of what happened during our stay in Logan. For instance, I'm not sure where we slept or how long we stayed. I do not even remember if I attended the actual funeral or what I wore to the gravesite. No matter how hard I try, I cannot pull these details back into my conscious mind.

What lingers as real is this: it was the first time I ever visited a gravesite, my dad did not make the trip with us, and I was overwhelmed by the onslaught of *New* I encountered. It is this overwhelming sense of all things foreign and new - of not belonging - that surfaces strongest of all in my memory.

I remember several times gathering with many of the cousins in one of my aunt's houses - a little, old white house built on a hill steeper than you'd imagine safely being able to build a house. There was a modest living room with a few worn couches and chairs, a simple kitchen and a little dining room. I remember multiple times walking outside in the frigid air to escape the suffocation of so much *New* - seeing the paint chips cracking off the siding, touching the metal fence around the perimeter of the yard, noting the run-down shed in the far corner - and feeling that everyone and everything was so strange.

The family shared meals all week, cousins corralling and learning about each other. My aunt's little home was jampacked with relatives and gobs of home-cooked food that friends and extended family had dropped off for the immediate family to eat. We waited in line with our Styrofoam plates and filled them with a bit of this and a bit of that. This was before the days when everyone had some sort of allergy or food intolerance (or at least before we knew that's what all the hives and cramps were about), before everything needed a "GF" or "DF" label, back when you used the same spoon to serve rows and rows of mysterious casserole dishes, making your best guess as to what was what and which would taste better.

During these family meals, conversation usually took a casual tone: people catching up on each other's lives, asking about the kids and jobs and how Great Aunt So-And-So was getting along, all of which only added to my sense of not belonging. Occasionally one of the cousins that lived close to my grandparents would share a memory of Pop, and it became obvious that theirs was a much deeper, knowing grief than what my siblings and I were facing. Then, sometimes, I would turn a corner and find two people lost in a tearful hug, and I'd know this was beyond my years.

Toward the end of the trip, the immediate family all gathered at my Pop's gravesite to scatter his ashes. I remember the family had waited and kept this a private ceremony just for his wife and children, and their children. It was dusk when we began our walk. Pop's plot was toward the front of an expansive, hillside cemetery located behind the high school that all of his children had attended. I don't think much was spoken that night, just lots of tears and quiet remembrance as the siblings scattered their father's ashes and tried to figure out how to say goodbye. I was relieved when we loaded up and headed back to our familiar, Georgia home.

~:~

Exactly two years later, as fate would have it, my family and I moved north to that small, foreign town in Ohio. We'd been living in a suburb of Atlanta for about a decade, where my parents had moved shortly after the birth of my older sister. My father had held a couple of jobs during that time, mostly in car sales or car sound system sales. My mother added to the family income by taking in several extra children a week. They hit particular financial hardships in the early 90's, which initially led my father to try to start his own business, but soon turned into financial disaster.

It was the bankruptcy that set the scene for the first time I ever remember seeing my father cry. This was also the second time I ever remember seeing my parents hug. In my memory, Grandma Leenie, my father's mom, had recently been down for a visit and a lot of emotions were stirring. Shortly after, I walked into that same oatmeal kitchen and saw my father now locked in my mother's embrace, crying.

It was later explained to me that my dad had a new job in Ohio and I vaguely understood that he also wanted to be closer to family. I secretly always sensed, though, that finally having had a son was the true catalyst for my father wanting to be nearer family again. Either way, he had moved to Ohio by mid-Fall to start a new job. The rest of the family followed just before the holidays.

We moved into the front half of my father's childhood home, where my parents still live to this day. It is a beautiful old white house with a large magnolia tree in the side yard. There is a huge front porch with a wide swing and a balcony with doors that connect to two of the upstairs bedrooms. When you walk in, you are greeted with rich brown, original woodwork on the floors, banisters and walls. There are several windows with original stained glass and beautiful iron lattice work. It is a masterpiece of a house.

That move landed us just blocks away from the hillside cemetery where my Pop's ashes had been scattered a couple short years earlier. It also landed us within viewing distance of that grand, old "high school on the hill," where my siblings and I would soon join generations of our family who had attended it. All the strange relatives, who on our previous trip caused me so much anxiety, would now become regular visitors and the people we would share our holidays with. All those foreign sights and sounds and smells that once told me I didn't belong, would now be called *home*.

~:~

I wonder often what my children will remember about their childhoods. Will they remember all the effort? All the special days? All the *"I love you's?"* Will they remember the smell of fresh paint from another Pinterest project brought to life? Will they recall the pattern of their favorite blanket or the feeling of their daddy's beard scratching them when they hug? Will they remember dance parties in the living room and walks around the neighborhood?

Like me, will they remember the first time they saw their mama cry? Crouched in a corner of their small kitchen; white cabinets and light aqua walls in the background, oak floors and crumbs underfoot, sun shining in the windows. Will they remember how I collapsed at the weight of grief, the weight of so many years of unanswered *"Why's?"* Will they recall how their tiny bodies huddled around me, with concern in their eyes, offering hands of comfort and warmth? How they asked, *"What's wrong mama?"* from the innocence of their years?

Will they remember how I sobbed and sobbed, until I finally caught my breath and called for help? How frantic I was? Will they recall how their father comforted me and calmed me, like only he could? Will they remember all the days I left to read or to write or to try to find some air that my lungs would accept? Will they remember that laughter still happened, but so did tears?

I wonder often what my children will remember about their childhoods. And I find that, *I hope they remember it all.*

Writing Prompt: Write about your earliest childhood memory - describe in as much detail as possible the sights, sounds, smells and souls of that moment.

BADGES

Although we often have a "merit badge" mentality, prayer shows us that we are actually "punished" by any expectation of merit or reward. For that expectation keeps us from the truly transformative experience called grace.
Richard Rohr, *Everything Belongs*

I'm looking at a photo of myself getting off the bus after my very first day of school. My face appears shyer than usual, a bit bashful and tentative, though still with a hint of mischief. This surprised me when I first studied the image, since I expected to see raw enthusiasm and joy. I know now that in the decade following that photo, school would become a haven for me of achievement and worth, friendship and belonging. I would find great value in being able to excel academically and a deep sense of identity in being a top student. I would have many battles to fight, certainly, but overall I would love even the awkward middle school years and the cliquey high school years.

But, from this photo, it seems I may have gotten off on the wrong foot.

My mother had outfitted me from head-to-toe in hot pink and aqua for the big day. My dress had a large collar with a bow on it, a big ruffle skirt with eyelet trim around the bottom, and "poofy" sleeves. As with all of my special occasion dresses, mom had sewn this especially for my first day of school, and I had anticipated the day I'd finally get to wear it. I wore white moccasins, complete with tassels, and pink ruffle socks folded over neatly at my ankles. My mother had pulled my long, golden hair into a high ponytail with a matching pink ribbon. I was equipped with a new, matching aqua book bag, slung sophisticatedly over one shoulder, and a well-stocked lunchbox.

At the time, our family lived in a suburb of Atlanta, called Stone Mountain. Our neighborhood was a typical cookie-cutter development, with only a couple different styles of houses making up the hundreds that neatly lined each street. Our modest, beige split-level was located on Pennybrook Court, just two blocks from the nearest bus stop and within viewing distance of it. With my mother, her entourage of babysitting kids and my two younger sisters in tow, my older sister and I began our walk to the bus stop.

In my adult mind, at first I remember the day as one filled with giddy anticipation. But with very vague living memories at my disposal, I resort to this solitary photo, snapped as I exited the school bus later that day. And instead of excitement, it alludes to a hesitation, an uncertainty that when I draw up my first living memory of school, I start to understand.

~:~

My first memory of being at school would have been well into the second week of classes. It was the first testing day, and soon I would learn how often and obtrusively these days came. My teacher was a severe-looking, African American woman, with a broad nose and stern eyebrows. She wore dark suits and short, salon-groomed hair. Her name was Mrs. Taylor.

Mrs. Taylor's face was a good indication of her character; she was strict and had little tolerance for unruly children. Having always been a rule-follower and a people pleaser, this shouldn't have been a problem for me. Tell me to sit still, and I wouldn't move a muscle. Tell me to sing the national anthem, and I'd try my hardest to remember every word. Tell me to cross my legs, and I'd let my feet go numb in obedience. Not at all that I was naturally compliant (because, that, I certainly wasn't) but I would do almost anything to gain the esteem and respect of those around me. And usually that meant following the rules.

However, there's only so much a six-year-old girl can do when all the rules she once knew get flipped upside down without notice, and the differences are never fully explained.

On this particular day of first grade, a neighborhood girlfriend was struggling with her math problems. She psst'ed for me to turn around and assist, which of course I did, as any well-mannered southern girl would. In the process of helping her, I was rudely interrupted by our teacher, who all but screamed at us, *"This is a test, children!"* Her outburst alarmed us, but still gave us no indication of what it was that we were doing wrong. We were well aware that this little sheet of paper was called a test. *And?* We stared at her blankly, I still turned around in my seat and resting on the friend's desk behind me. Perhaps it was our lack of inaction or our blank stares, or perhaps it was just the end of a very long week for Mrs. Taylor. Whatever it was, the next thing we knew, both my friend and I were in the principal's office *being sent home for cheating.*

I remember being so innocently grief-stricken by the severity of the discipline I was now receiving, having so unknowingly committed this terrible offense. I sobbed and sobbed as I waited in the hard plastic chair of the school office for my mother to come pick me up. I could see my neighborhood girlfriend down the aisle of red chairs, sitting sullenly at the opposite end (of course they had separated us trouble-makers, lest we conspire toward some additional mischief!). I was torn between terrible sadness and a faint sense of injustice.

That day, Mrs. Taylor showed her students loud and clear that she - and so, we presumed, the world, too - had a zero tolerance policy for rule-breakers, whether you knew which rules you were breaking or not. She was preparing us for a lifetime of "do this" and "be this or else," and I'd gotten the message. It would serve me extremely well in my academic career. So well that I cannot recall a single other instance of "misbehavior" at school over the next twelve years. I wonder, now, if that experience launched me into a life of performing, concealing and people-pleasing. I wonder if that was the day this message was sealed into my young heart: *You are only as good as others say you are.*

First grade came and went without further hiccup. In second grade, I was placed in the beautiful Mrs. Copeland's class. I took to her, and she to me, immediately. She was everything Mrs. Taylor was not: short, slight, feminine, kind. She had a beautiful smile and wore lively, youthful dresses. By this time, I'd learned all the appropriate rules and had modified my behavior accordingly. I was the model student and Mrs. Copeland adored me.

I remember often asking Mrs. Copeland for extra assignments. I was both intelligent and ambitious, and was quickly becoming aware of the attention and worth I could gain in being an over-achiever. I helped Mrs. Copeland with special projects, did extra credit work constantly and was the student chosen nearly any time there needed to be a class representative. I became such a favorite that Mrs. Copeland had me come spend a weekend with her near the end of the school year. We went out for pizza, played with her young son, and I got to learn first-hand the world of African American hair. I felt warm and welcomed and well-esteemed with Mrs. Copeland.

Honor Roll and Student of the Month became defining labels in second grade. I'd learned that pizza and prizes, attention and smiles, were attached to such achievements. It was also in second grade that I was tested and placed in a special program called T.A.G.: Talented and Gifted (I now realize how harmful this label is when used with selectivity). T.A.G. was a once-a-week class that took just a few kids out of our normal classrooms for an afternoon and allowed us to engage with a smaller group of students in more explorative, in-depth projects. We were given special resources, took extra field trips and got to carry the pride of another valued label. I started to live for earning these labels, like badges on a Girl Scout sash, signs of my capability and worth.

It was also in second grade that I began to learn the value of beauty and the power it held over others. I was a pretty girl who carried herself with poise and confidence, so I soon became the object of affection for some of the boys in my class. Joshua Benson was one such boy, slim, dark hair, veering toward the nerdy table before it existed. He brought me gifts and invited me over for play dates. He gave me a special Valentine and lavished me with extra attention. It wouldn't be long before Pretty Girl and Class Crush became badges I pinned on with pride as well.

With all these badges I entered third grade, shoulders back, chin up. However, my luck took a turn for the worse with another stern, unhappy teacher. Mrs. Edwards was very round, had short, frizzy hair and wore long, flowing skirts every day. I remember daydreaming about all the games we could play with the yards of fabric at our disposal in those awful skirts. There was no specific incident that caused my distaste for Mrs. Edwards, perhaps just that she was such a letdown after the adored Mrs. Copeland. I did, however, continue to thrive academically, was active in the T.A.G. program and won my first school-wide honor for writing an Arbor Day poem that was published in the local newspaper.

Year after year, things proceeded just the same. I earned my badges faithfully: Honors Student, Class Representative, Teacher's Pet. I went to all sorts of leadership camps, won writing awards and was always in advanced courses. I was a cheerleader and competitive swimmer, dated many of the "popular" boys, volunteered at food banks and Special Olympics and nursing homes. I did quite a bit of public speaking and became very active in my church. I was on the homecoming court, graduated as Valedictorian of my high school and was voted Most Likely to Succeed. *With each badge, I felt myself more solidly defined; I lived and breathed the euphoria of achievement.*

As a child and then well into my teenage years, my identity and worth became so tied up in being a top student and pleasing everyone around me that I became a prisoner to others' expectations. I was subconsciously imprisoned by the need to follow the rules and please those around me. It wasn't any longer a matter of being a *"Talented and Gifted"* student; I was a *"Tailored and Good"* student. I was bound by all the badges I'd earned over the years. I smiled often, sucked in constantly and worked hard to do all I felt was expected of me.

~:~

Only recently have I become aware of how deeply those badges were pinned into my very heart. I've learned the problem with labels; the problem with being so clearly defined and having earned so many badges is that your true self becomes constricted by it all. The badges aren't just pins you wear on your sash, they are stabbed into your heart and become a part of who you are. I was known as capable, so I had to be capable. I was known as smart, so I had to get good grades. I was known as pretty, so I constantly dieted and exercised and generally obsessed over my appearance, hoping the end result would be pretty *enough*. And I was so used to leading and being able and knowing the answers that, at least emotionally, I had no idea how to ask for help. Anne Lamott puts it well when she says in her book *Stitches*:

> *The American way is to not need help, but to help. One of the hardest lessons I had to learn was that I was going to need a lot of help, and for a long time. What saved me was that I found gentle, loyal and hilarious companions, which is at the heart of meaning: maybe we don't find a lot of answers to life's tougher questions, but if we find a few true friends, that's even better.*

Since so many of my friends were in their own adolescent prisons at the time, it'd be years before companionship would provide true relief and even longer before I'd begin to understand the need to say, *"Help!"* once in a while. I am learning now, slowly, practicing the awkward act of confessing that I can't do it all alone. And I am blessed to have found a couple friendships like Lamott describes: gentle and faithful and true people who are themselves pursuing freedom and wholeness. I cling to these friends and thank God for them.

Today, looking at this photo of myself after my first day of school, I cannot help but wish the younger me would have failed more. I wish she would have bombed a test here or there or missed a deadline every once in a while. I wish she would have asked her questions and broken the rules and let others down - and learned that the world wouldn't crumble just because of it, *that she wouldn't crumble because of it.* I wish someone would have said, *"Stop! Take a break. You don't have to prove anything."*

That little girl is older now, here in me. And the best I can do today is hold her gently, bravely. I can help her rip off the badges and then hold my hand over all the wounds they've left. I can tell her the truth. I can tell her, *"It's okay. You're just enough, just as you are."* I can applaud her efforts. I can let her rest and laugh and dance. I can be kind to her when she tries and fails. I can love her for doing nothing at all.

Writing Prompt: Write about your earliest memory of school. Perhaps, like me, you will need to refer back to images and other memorabilia to help gather the details. Consider: *Who was that child?* Was school a place of belonging or a place of pain? What badges did you earn over the years and what has that meant for your life today?

WHY & I

The great artists ... help us to know that we are often closer to God in our doubts than in our certainties, that it is all right to be like the small child who constantly asks: Why? Why? Why?
Madeleine L'Engle, *Walking on Water*

I have often asked, *"Why?"* As a young child, I remember many times standing before my mother, as if in face-to-face combat, readied for battle, whining or screaming or hissing, *"Why?!"* My mother - my over-worked, always-sacrificing, fully-stretched mother - with five kids of her own, a full-time job and a house to maintain, would sigh beneath my constant questioning.

I remember the innate need to *understand* pulsing up through my throat, the pushing back, the longing to feel truth and meaning flowing through every vein of life. My hungry, youthful eyes would search and search, observing every move of those around me, looking for truth in it all. *I was a child that needed to know.*

I remember, too, an innocent decoration, given as a gift from my father's mother to my mom, haunting me and taunting me and causing my blood pressure as a child to rise in rage. It was a ridiculous little hen, of barn red and country cream, mounted on the window sill above our kitchen sink. Five baby chicks hung from the hen's belly, representing each of my mother's five children. The inscription read, *"I'm the mom, that's why!"* My mother quoted Mrs. Hen often. She loved that hen for the rightful authority it gave her, but I absolutely despised Mrs Hen. She sung to me, not of parental authority and safety, but of silence and shutting down, of façades and running away.

I remember well moments of discipline, moments when I'd pushed one too many times, when my questioning became too much and my weary mother would refuse another word. In those days, the *"Why?"* was called "back-talk," a punishable offense of disrespect and obstinance - and so I was often labeled a disrespectful, obstinate child. Popular parenting books also labeled my temperament as "strong-willed" and my mother, not being "strong-willed" herself, read and tried to understand and deal with her Why-child as best she could. As a mother now, I empathize with her struggle, her effort and her fatigue. But then, I was simply wild with *"Why's"* and furious for justice and truth and meaning. *I was a child that needed to know.*

I can picture clearly that light oak kitchen of my childhood, Mrs. Hen haunting me from her perch, myself steadied upon a countertop, around the age of eight. It was another stand-off, my mother on the other side of the kitchen. I have no recollection of what we were arguing about, only that this accusation, given repeatedly by then, finally broke through: *"Stop talking back! You don't always have to have the last word!"* It felt like a curse, a call to silence, to refuse the questioning, justice-driven me. All of the sudden *"Why?"* tasted awful.

I ran away that night. In the scuffle of the stand-off and with the echoing of *"Stop talking back!"* ringing in my ears, my heart ran for space - ran for all the *"Why's"* still lingering in my heart. I brought a couple blankets and a snack and nestled myself in the woods behind our Georgia home. It was warm and comfortable and I stayed there through dusk. I intended to stay there forever.

As darkness increased, in the moonlit sky and in my own soul, I wilted at the thought of forever. I squirmed in my skin – my own damaged, obstinate, Why-wailing skin. I felt labeled, broken, misshaped and unwanted. And so I spit *"Why?"* out that night, stomped it into the dirt, made mud and hoped it would harden for good.

~:~

I see now that when I ran away at eight it was not just a casual childhood experience of defiance or adventure. It was not a quickly forgotten night, an escapade of youth, but rather a defining moment in my life. That night, I ran both from myself and all the *"Why's."* I began my tormented fleeing from and clinging to the Why-child, the struggle to feel both comfortable in my own skin and accepted by those around me.

In my teenage years, there were days the "back-talk" gained force and stamina. But increasingly often, the beating of justice in my heart was squelched and the dissident voice within was silenced. The child that needed to know sat crouched in the corner, never to be silenced completely, but much louder now was the teenager that needed to *belong*, that craved words of praise and worth and rightness of being. *My passion became appearing right, not doing right; performing for praise, not fighting for answers.*

When, at thirteen, my heart awakened to the presence of Divine Love, I was momentarily reunited with the Why-child. I marveled at the thought of an acceptance of all of me, *"Why's"* and all. So much of my insecurity was scooped up and answered in that Love; the need to be valued and esteemed were met in Father.

But within a year of conversion, I started to see the cracks, the remaining *"Why's"* that Love hadn't fully healed or answered or taken away in an instant, and I broke at the hopelessness of it all. I remember discovering Nichole Nordeman's song, *To Know You,* and weeping at her soul-cry, **my** *soul-cry: "Be patient with my doubt, I'm just trying to figure out Your will."* It seemed Divine Love, too, judged and accused and shamed me into a corner. It seemed my *"Why's",* even here, were foul and unwanted.

And so the façades of pleasing people and wearing a smile were soon erected again, just a bit wiped down and with a Jesus-fish sticker in the corner. As a Christian, I found meaning again in following the rules and silencing the questions. *"Why?"* was just as foul-tasting a word and just as much a part of me - a foul, unwanted part of me. Again I felt broken and misshaped - *if only I could silence the Why-child once and for all.*

The struggle ebbed and flowed throughout the next decade. I would find level ground for years, with only the faintest nagging of falsity, only to eventually find myself back in a corner of shame and despair and self-hate. I would run away from my faith multiple times, feeling that all the *"Why's"* were too much, that Love had no room for seekers, that a "believer" with so much uncertainty was not welcome. And I so *longed* to be welcomed.

For years, it seemed impossible that a foul thing like *"Why?"* could coexist with Love. From time to time, I would become aware that some part of me was being suffocating, and I would muster all the courage, and stand up for my true self. I would embrace the Why-child briefly, hide with her and dry her tears. But every time, when her cries would quiet and her straining would stop, when the sobbing calmed and the muscles relaxed, I would walk away, façades in hand. I would walk away from her again, and again. I would live the rules and check the boxes and be the smile. *I would silence the questions and speak the "truth;" I would recite the answers, not realizing I was living a lie.*

Then, finally, life would take my breath away. Pain and loss would back me into a corner with the Why-child, and force me to sit with her and to listen. Feebly, I would reach for the façades, the masks, the false selves. I would long for the comfort of having the answers, of being accepted, of fitting in and being right. I would reach, but this time, I was too weak.

~:~

It took over three years of sitting, often in tears, mostly in silence, with the Why-child before I began to accept her as me. Slowly, I would learn to be my own worth, to refuse the labels and the shallow relationships. I would find the courage to stand up and fight again - for the Why-child, for me, for mystery and questions that needed asked, and for life. I would stand apart from the crowd and tell my story. It would be messy and painful and beautiful and freeing all at once.

And I would find my way to other Why-children, too, and there learn to love, to embrace, even to call "Why?" beautiful. I'd read page after page, finally feeling at home, finally feeling welcomed whole. They'd say, "*Questions, no matter how shocking or blasphemous or arrogant or ignorant or raw, are rooted in humility. A humility that understands that I am not God. And there is more to know. Questions bring freedom. Freedom that I don't have to be God and I don't have to pretend to have it all figured out. I can let God be God.*"[1]

I would sit with these words, marveling, and think, *You mean it is okay to wonder? You mean there are others that need to know, too? You mean all the asking was beautiful and holy all along?* I would sigh heavily, freed.

Every time, I would find myself breathing deeper and freer, these brave words filling my heart with hope. I'd rise from the corner, holding the Why-child's hand gently in mine, and being learning of the beauty of mystery. I'd read to her truth from our kin: "*People who want life hammered down into tight, legalistic certainties seem to me to be the people most insecure inside. Frankly, the folks who frighten me the most are those who are dead certain about everything, who have all the answers and no questions. Have we Christians forgotten the transforming value of a question? There's an art to living your questions. You peel them. You*

---

[1] *Velvet Elvis*, Rob Bell

listen to them. You let them spawn new questions. You hold the unknowing inside. You linger with it instead of rushing into half-baked answers.[2]

With care and whispered reminders: *"The mystery is the truth"* and, *"Live the questions"* and, most often, *"You are courageous, you are enough,"* I'd lead the Why-child back into the Light, where she always belonged.

Writing Prompt: Write about the most memorable disagreement you have ever had with your parents (or other authority figure). What was at the heart of the argument? What was brought to life or squelched in that experience?

---

[2] *When the Heart Waits*, Sue Monk Kidd

AND

I have lived the runner, panting ahead in worry, pounding back in regrets, terrified to live in the present, because here-time asks me to do the hardest thing of all: just open wide and receive.
Ann Voskamp, *One Thousand Gifts*

"Maybe you love your kids a little too much!" she said over her shoulder as she left our house that day. She waved a sweet goodbye, this dear friend who had no kids of her own and, so, I concluded, had no idea what she was talking about. She spoke in jest, as comments like these often are, just sort of throwing her two cents out into the wind. But no sooner had her casual comment found its way into the air, then did it find its way right into the back of my head, crashing, bruising, leaving me dizzy.

The target was my affection and perceived over-protection of my little ones - in other words, *my heart.* I was able to shake the accusation off in the moment, but soon learned that her words had stuck, had lodged into my parenting file and kept pricking at my conscience.

If you're a parent and have ever had a non-parent comment on how well you are doing, you know it can be crazy-making. It doesn't seem to matter the context or the tone, if the speaker was compassionate or on crack. It's about *your* parenting, how well you are caring for your most prized possessions, so it keeps on pricking and poking and annoying you until you find a way to lay it to rest. Or am I the only crazy one?

Driving to the grocery store later that same day, I was somewhat successfully listening to a radio show on NPR. Of all things, the guest speaker, Jennifer Senior, was a researcher and author of the book, *All Joy, No Fun*. The book focuses on the effects that children have on their parents.

I tuned in just as Senior started describing shifts in parenting behaviors and styles over the past few decades and how dramatically we have switched to a very child-focused orientation. She referenced protestors in the 1920's and 30's fighting to end child labor in America and how their battle cry was, effectively, *"Children are delicate, precious; they're our most prized possessions."* This was in stark contrast to previous worldviews, which often saw children only as assets insofar as they could contribute economically to the household. Children were once considered personal property, not prized possessions. But this all changed early last century.

There were all sorts of studies being referenced and historical facts being cited as to how this switch has not been *all* positive. Research about parenting becoming a world that revolves around children, children being overindulged and under-prepared for real world problems, and so on. It was hard to piece all the comments together between the constant, *"Hey, Mama's,"* coming from my backseat passengers and the fact that I was driving on half-plowed snowy roads. I heard just enough, though, for my parenting red flag to shoot up in alarm.

The pricking and the poking of that earlier, *"Maybe you love them too much"* comment now increased with a fury. I thought, *"Oh no! She is talking to me. This is about as close as it comes to God parting the clouds and speaking these days. Maybe it's true; maybe I'm ruining them. Maybe I do love them too much!"*

With a little less toddler taunting being thrown at me from behind and a couple hours to sit with my thoughts, I came back with a much more balanced revelation: *I was only sort of screwing my kids up.* I saw myself rallying to be their biggest fan and best friend, raising Happiness as the highest goal. I saw my dreams of self-confident, self-aware kids being built on more quality time with *me.* I saw all the "mama dates" and cuddles and kisses and endless playtime, and wondered if it was a bit misdirected.

And then - thanks to Brené Browns' book, *Gift of Imperfections* - I gave myself some grace, some more space, and took a long, deep breath.

~:~

This seems to be the story of my life: swinging wildly from one extreme to the other, trying always to find some semblance of balance in the middle. Because the truth is, I do absolutely adore my children. They are two and three and are already the most amazing people on the planet. Seriously. They are funny, bright, kind, creative. They are witty and resilient, playful and brave. Yes, I know, I'm their mama so of course I think that. But this time it's all true. Just ask my husband.

I'm fortunate that I love and *like* my kids (most of the time, that is, but I'm getting ahead of myself). I transitioned to staying home with them full-time when they were almost one and almost two. Before that transition, I would often cry during my drive home from the office at the thought of all the little moments I had missed that day. Sometimes I would get so twisted up about it, I'd have a hard time really enjoying them once I was finally home. I resisted making evening plans and never went on dates with my husband. I wanted our weekends free and I wanted every second I wasn't in the office to be 100% focused attention on my babies. I hated anything, and sometimes anyone, that took an ounce of my time away from my little ones (see what I mean about extremes).

Even as I write this, I hesitate to express how strongly I longed to be home with my children for two reasons. First, because I know it sounds extreme and obsessive and not at all like so many popular parenting blogs and books today that constantly seem to bemoan what a pain in the ass their kids can be. Choosing to quit my job and stay home with my kids, and genuinely loving it, is not the culturally cool thing to feel or say these days. It's certainly not the standard water-cooler confession. I'm afraid I'll be labeled a weirdo or categorized into some forbidden, old-fashioned box. And I'm not at all interested in more parenting judgments. I already know, *I love them too much.*

The second reason I hesitate is because I know many adoring moms that don't at all feel the way I do about being at home with their kids all day. I'm not sure all the differences, but I assume it is some mix of personality and career aspirations and our own childhoods, which is to say that it's a huge decision and can be affected by lots of factors. I don't know why I feel so strongly this way and others feel so strongly the other - about parenting or anything else. But I'm comfortable saying that we each have our own story and have to live out our roles as authentically, lovingly and bravely as we know how. And for me that looks like being home with my kids and, maybe, for you it doesn't. Truth and love are what matters.

~:~

As I write this, I am exactly a year into the whole stay-at-home mom gig and feel like I am finally filling back up all those vats that felt so empty from missing the dailies of my children's first years. We cuddle, I give them a kiss or hug every other second or two. I tell them I love them about a dozen times a day, usually followed by an adoring, *"You're so kind."* or *"You're amazing."* I breathe in their scrumptious softness and thank them for letting me spend the day with them. I'm mindfully grateful that I get to be a part of discovering the world with them day in and day out. I really, really love my kids and I really like them, too.

But, it's - *no* - AND, it's hard. Even adoring them so much and really liking them a lot and feeling this intense sense of gratitude - even all that sometimes isn't enough to make cleaning up the third poopy-pants mess in an hour worth it. I, like you, get so irritated when my kid acts like he didn't hear the command I just yelled at him 14 times, despite my volume, despite my tone, despite his sister crying hysterically right beside him. I squeeze arms too tightly in my frustration and hurry to get out the door. I pretend to be listening with lots of *"mmhmm's"* but am often spaced out or preoccupied with my own thoughts. I hate potty-training just as much as the next parent. I dread mealtime, which at our house is an endless chorus of *"Stay in your seat!"* and *"Don't throw your food!"* I'm often unsure how to discipline effectively and am pathetically inconsistent. Many days I feel bored and brain-dead, especially in the winter. Every single day, I'm thrilled when it's nap time.

See - *phew!* - I'm really very normal. *I adore my kids* AND *they drive me nuts.*

I got a wonderfully healthy dose of this phenomenon during a playdate recently. One of my dearest friends was visiting for the day with her two littles. Miraculously, all four kids were on the same nap schedule, so we had very high hopes of hours of relaxing conversation on the couch with our hot coffee and cozy pants. The kids played well all morning, ate big lunches and were even asking to go to sleep once nap time came around. It looked like our dreams of coffee and conversation were well within reach. We parted ways for final potty breaks and books before bed, then plopped back down together on the couch with a sigh and a grin. *Good job, Mama!*

Before either of us could speak a word, the first child cried out. She was distraught that she didn't get to close brother's door by herself and wanted a do-over. The do-over was refused, which caused more wailing, which required soft words and a few songs. Ten minutes later we met up again, in silence and relief, and poured our coffee.

With sips of hot coffee on our tongues, the second child cried out. This one had removed his pull-up and was now walking around the hallways half-naked. Apparently this was a defective pull-up that was so scratchy, the child couldn't sleep. But he could pee. All over his bed. Blankets were swapped, clothes were changed and the child was resettled. Fifteen minutes later and now with a heavier sigh akin to, *"Golly these kids sure are a lot of work!"* we plopped together on the couch, still grasping at hope that an adult conversation would take place. No kidding, a split second after our rears made contact with cushion, child number three called out from her room, *"I'm still hungry! Mama, I'm hungry."* Perhaps prompted by this outburst, child number two began singing loudly and kicking the wall. We rolled our eyes and heaved the heaviest sigh yet, a *"Now I'm gonna kill 'em!"* sigh, then went to settle, soothe and sing again.

We did, finally, get to relax together and finish our cups of coffee - about 45 minutes after originally pouring them. We ended up having a deeply connecting conversation and laughed together at the joys and trials of motherhood. We reminisced on our college days together, how much we took our freedom for granted, how ignorant and naive we were. *And how we would not trade these days of parenting our littles for anything in the world.* All four kids slept simultaneously for almost an hour as we sipped and talked and enjoyed each second.

The littlest woke up first, all rosy-cheeked and fuzzy. Soon after, my two awoke, crazy haired and warmed to the core. The last wandered out shortly afterwards, cozying up on the couch with the rest of us. We welcomed our groggy kids with big open arms and gentle cuddles, and started our mama work all over again.

~:~

I didn't understand the AND of parenting very well before staying at home full-time. I was too overcome with missing the kids and obsessing about their well-being while I was gone. But now, after a year of messy meals and poopy pants, defiant toddlers and cranky babies, I get it. Writing about that day with the nap time fiasco put AND into perspective so clearly for me. The adoration AND the irritation. The affection AND the exhaustion. We loved our kids and played and laughed and soaked them up AND we longed for them to go away, go to sleep, leave us alone. *And.*

Long after this contemplation of AND began, I came across a quote by author and psychologist Charles L. Whitfield. He says, *"In recovery, we begin to learn that most things in our life, including our recovery, are not all-or-none, not either-or. Rather, they are both-and. They have shades of gray, they are somewhere in the middle, a "3, 4, 5, 6, or 7" and not either a '0' or a '10.'"* This middle ground, *both-and* space is the kind of parent I hope to be.

When I remember that initial accusation, months in the past now, I momentarily become an unsure school girl, wavering unsteadily in my role as a mother. I find myself regularly fighting the pricks and pokes - of overindulgence, of loving too much - aimed right at my heart. Sometimes in an effort to appease the pricks, I make my three-year-old clean his room all by himself or I tell my daughter *"No"* for no other reason than to teach her to accept that word as a real and complete answer. I encourage my son to keep trying his hand at something rather than butting in and doing it for him. I shoo them both away for alone play. These, so far, are my best efforts at finding balance.

Still, I kiss them a hundred times a day and tell them often how amazing they are. I cuddle them close before bed, lavish them with tender kisses and sing about how much I love them. I remind them what a privilege I consider it to be to get to spend my days with them. Then I turn off the lights, shut their doors, and hope to God they sleep for at least ten hours.

Writing Prompt: Where in your life have you limited yourself by *either-ors*? Consider your career aspirations, your parenting, your relationships, your identity and your spirituality. Write about what AND does, or would, look like in your life.

LIFE IN 3D

Because the art, the task, the challenge, the invitation of the
spiritual life is for you to see the depths of your own life. For
you to see the Divine Presence in everything you do.
This is where the action is: Learning to see.

Rob Bell, *Receipts*

I recently had this random idea that the kids and I needed to watch *Mary Poppins*. It's not a movie that I have any nostalgic attachment to or even a particular appreciation for. It was more like a pregnancy craving that came out of nowhere and instinctively needed to be satiated, like midnight runs for pickles and peanut butter and olives.

As a family, we do not own many movies. The couple dozen DVDs that we do have on hand are mostly gifts or hand-me-downs. There are a few true favorites in the lot, like *Shawshank Redemption* and *Pride and Prejudice*. But, mostly, it's an eclectic mix that only gets utilized once in a blue moon when my husband and I are simultaneously bored, available and in the mood. Kind of like sex.

Every now and then I'm tempted to beef up our movie selection, but there are two major things working against this move. First, we have somehow managed to own an old $20 DVD player *without a remote* for the past several years. This means that we can never skip previews, we can never fast forward or rewind, turn off subtitles or watch the special features. This also means that we've seen the first twenty minutes of every kid movie we own a million times - *and still have no idea how they end.*

For instance, from *Ratatouille*, the Pixar movie about a budding five star chef trapped inside a rat's body, I could recite line for line the opening conversations between rat-chef Remy and his older brother. I could recount with detail the first time Remy cooks, what he makes, how the kitchen is set up, who says what...but after that soup scene, I'm lost. Who becomes friends with whom? Will Remy ever accept his life as a rat? Or will the world ever accept Remy as a chef? These are things that only privileged remote-control-owners could know. Not me.

Twice now we have gotten a "Universal Remote," with the intentions of once and for all righting our remote-less DVD player situation. Of these two purchases, one was with our own money and one was a gift. (Yes, a family member equally as cheap and absurd as us actually bought my husband a Universal Remote as a birthday present this year). We read directions thoroughly, asked the sage father-in-law to try his hand at it, but, still, neither remote would connect. We were left to conclude that either our DVD player was too ancient to fit the term "Universal," or that this was another instance of false advertising. Nobody ever thought of just buying a new DVD player.

It seems normal now to start a movie fifteen or twenty minutes before we're ready to sit down and watch it, thus avoiding the previews the old-fashioned way. It's become a fun guessing game as to whether the captions will be turned on this time or not. And, other than the fact that my kids may have a confused sense of plot, climax and resolution, we've coped quite well with no remote. Still, the incentive to invest in new DVDs is obviously quite low.

The second thing that causes me to pause when I'm tempted to purchase a movie or two is the astonishing availability of movies online. I'm not talking about Netflix or some other subscription-based movie service, although we were briefly members of one. I'm talking about the simplicity of typing "Mary Poppins full movie free" into Google and finding a dozen sites with the full movie available online. Occasionally there are requirements on these sites, sometimes for money, but usually just for personal information. *I never use these sites.* And occasionally, there are sites with obnoxious, even x-rated advertisements. *I never use these sites, either.* If you keep digging, maybe to page two of your Google search, you can almost always find a site with no strings attached and no skimpy clothes. We do a good bit of our movie viewing through these backdoor sites.

Now, there was a day, back when everything in life was clearly black or white - and I did my damnedest to stay within the white - that I would have considered such backdoor movie viewings a crime and a sin. I was so tightly wound up about always doing what was "right" that I would become soul-sick with myself for putting an item down in a store in the wrong place, or I would fall into a pit of repentance for not tipping exactly 15%. I remember once I was panic stricken when I realized halfway home that I had received more change than was owed. I turned around and frantically returned the over-payment to an amused and confused cashier. Some may praise this sort of behavior as honesty or integrity, but for me, it was more of a legalistic prison.

Since those right-obsessed days, life has delivered me a lot of grays. In the face of loss, death, betrayal and loneliness, being right takes a bit of a backseat. Surviving is all that really matters - and then living with love and honesty, but not with an insane list of rules. My obsession with being defined as a "good girl" finally (mostly) has left center stage. Now, I usually keep the overpaid change and use it as my personal coffee fund. I tip beyond the recommended percentages, because I remember what it was like to be a struggling college student. I give my unwanted items to the cashier on good days, and throw them on any old shelf on the more frenzied days, free of shame.

And, I regularly watch movies illegally.

There were many sites offering the full length version of Mary Poppins, so I found the first one with no strings attached and cuddled up with the kids. The quality wasn't great, forcing us to choose between a blurry full screen view or a clearer, but much tinier, view. Both had their cons, but we're not media snobs around here (remember that old DVD player?), so we happily settled for the blurry full screen view. I consoled myself with the thought that perhaps half the viewing audience in the '60s was dealing with some blurry screen issues themselves, unlike our HD,

Bluray, blahblahblah technology of today. So, really, ours was just a more historically accurate viewing experience.

Kyler and Havyn were amused by all the magic and silliness and loved it when the father, Mr. Banks, bangs his head on the fireplace in bewilderment at Mary Poppins' arrival. They immediately took to all the singing and dancing and soon attached to Jane and Michael, the young children of the Banks' household whom Mary Poppins nannies. Whenever there was a scene without the children, Havyn would incessantly implore, *"Mama, where that girl at?"* until finally she reappeared. They hummed songs, asked questions and retold their favorite scenes the rest of the week.

In thirty minute spurts over a couple days, we made it through almost the entire movie. Most of it felt like a first-time viewing for me. I laughed with the kids at silly Uncle Albert and his gravity-reversing jokes. I admired the beauty and poise of Mary Poppins on her stroll through the park with Bert and appreciated the color and liveliness carried through every scene. I felt myself sinking into the couch in utter calm when Mary sings *"Tuppence a Bag"* and oohing and aahhing at the chimney sweeps as they perform their rooftop piece. Throughout, I judged Mr. and Mrs. Banks with the old black-and-white me, shaping the severest furled brow I could manage whenever they appeared on screen.

If you are unfamiliar with *Mary Poppins*, as I was, here is my 30 second summary. The Banks are an affluent British family, the father a banker and the wife busied with political activism. There are two children, cared for by a hired nanny, only one of several household employees. Mr. and Mrs. Banks come across as extremely consumed with their causes: Mr. Banks is intent on utter propriety and making as much money as possible, while Mrs. Banks is determined to *"Get the Vote"* for women. Both are nearly oblivious to their children, Jane and Michael. They cycle through nannies on a weekly or monthly basis, delegating every aspect of their children's care to another. There seems to be little affection, or interaction, between parent and child.

Now, I usually say that being the mother of two toddlers is the most humbling experience in the world. You realize, yet again, that you're only sort of in control, and often not at all. You realize that no matter how "right" you do it all, things go wrong and get messy and tantrums happen at ear-splitting volume in the middle of the library. You learn the beauty and the disaster of free will, and you spend your days trying desperately to keep everyone uninjured, mostly happy and somewhat clean. Parenting toddlers is a humbling adventure that has put my pre-mama judgments in their rightful place.

Yet, something about the Banks' apparent oblivion to their children's needs, and what came across as their total lack of nurturing and affection got my inner Judge Judy roaring. I listened to them sing-song their philosophies on raising a family and all but snarled in response. I was aghast realizing that mealtime, playtime and even bedtime were responsibilities delegated away from the parents, to nannies that were often strangers to the Banks family. I could barely watch when the children politely stood before their father to say *"Good night,"* then went back upstairs with the nanny - stoic, proper, restrained. I stared wide-eyed as Mrs. Banks asks a dirty chimney sweep she's just met to watch Jane and Michael while she heads hurriedly to a rally. I tilted my glasses down, furled my brow even further and shook a disapproving finger at Mr. and Mrs. Banks, as if to say, *"Shame on you. I would never!"*

~:~

Later that week, when it came time to sit down and give myself to the habit of writing I've been working so hard to establish in my life, I felt brittle and empty. Initially, I was so distracted that it seemed all but impossible to get more than three coherent lines down on paper. My mind wandered and the cursor blinked on an empty screen. I went through my usual list of excuses and had just about convinced myself that sitting in front of the computer any longer would be a total waste of time, when the image of Mary's carpetbag popped into my head. I saw sweet, proper Mary place her large carpetbag on her bedroom table and then, magically, begin pulling out all sorts of impossible items. As Jane and Michael stare in wonder, Mary pulls out a large mirror, then an ornate lamp, a coatrack and a large house plant. With each item, the children inspect under the table and inside the bag, trying to figure out where everything is coming from. At one point, Michael's amazement reaches saturation and he says in his beautiful British accent, *"But, Mary, the bag was just empty!"* to which Mary simply gives a sweet, sly glance and then continues on. She puts her hand into the empty carpetbag, shuffles all sorts of things around for a while, bumps and huffs and finally pulls out her measuring tape, with a *"Hmpf"* that seems to say, *"I knew it was in there somewhere!"*

I see Mary and her carpetbag - the impossible coming to be, the empty full of much - and know there is truth for my soul here. I listen as that carpetbag sings to me a song of possibility and becoming, even out of emptiness. I hear an urging that if I would just plant myself at a table and reach my hand in, *deep inside myself,* something would be there. Even though I'd looked and looked before, inspected and felt around and was *sure* my soul was empty, something would still come out. Magically, mysteriously, but certainly, there were impossible somethings waiting to be pulled out, even of me. I would probably need to bump and shuffle and huff a bit to find them, but eventually I could hmpf an *"I knew it was in there somewhere!"* And, hopefully, in the end, I would be able to sit back in awe at the impossible something that came forth - just as the kids and I sat in awe at all that came forth from Mary's magically-empty-yet-totally-full carpetbag.

I sat at the computer a while longer that evening. I channeled my inner Mary Poppins - that light, mysterious, beautiful side we all have. I wrote and huffed a bit and reached around for a while. I stood in stubbornness and determination, willing myself to believe for impossible somethings and for more than meets the eye. It was not nearly as magical as I had hoped, and there were no catchy songs playing in the background. I was not dressed in a lovely white corseted dress and no magical winds came to carry me to fantastical places. It was work staying in Marymode, and I didn't look nearly so graceful and beautiful doing it.

And yet, eventually, something did come forth, out of my emptiness. I found words buried deep within, words that told more of the story of me, that wove meaning and memory into these days so quickly passing. I gained a treasure of true knowing. I learned, at least for a night, that even when something looks empty, even when we're sure someone has nothing to say - that we ourselves have nothing worth saying, nothing to give, nothing of value or uniqueness to offer the world around us - we just haven't looked long or hard enough. I learned to *keep looking, to hold close the mystery that things aren't always what they seem.*

~:~

This truth: *things aren't always what they seem,* continued to ring through my consciousness. A few days after watching *Mary Poppins* with the kids, a friend casually, serendipitously mentioned the movie, *Saving Mr. Banks.* I am generally so out of touch with pop culture that movie titles rarely conjure up any context for me. I haven't lived with cable for over a decade and I could count on both hands how many times I've been to a movie theater *in my life.* If that weren't enough, don't forget that our DVD player doesn't even have a remote control. I'm not exactly a media-guru.

Naturally, then, the movie title initially slid right past me. Somewhere in my subconscious, though, the name grabbed hold and later on I realized that perhaps this Mr. Banks could be the same now-despised, inept father Mr. Banks, the object of my recent scorn and judgments - *the* Mr.

Banks of *Mary Poppins*. I did a quick search online and found that, yes, the men were one-and-the-same. The cravings I'd had to watch *Mary Poppins* earlier in the week now paled in light of these new urges to view *Saving Mr. Banks*. I found myself uncharacteristically giddy and eager for evening to come so that I could find the movie online and watch it (which I did, illegally).

The film did not disappoint. With Mary's words still fresh in my mind - *things aren't always what they seem* - and my own judgment of the Banks still alive and deep, I sat enthralled, ashamed, awakened. I watched as P.L. Travers, the author of the book *Mary Poppins*, struggles to give up the rights to her dear Mary and the Banks family for film production. Walt Disney personally pursues Travers for over twenty years, trying to gain the rights, developing an entire film script in the hopes of finally wooing her to sign. This pursuit is interspersed with a raw retelling of Travers' own childhood - the story of a young girl who adores her ill father, watches him die and carries the weight, the responsibility, the pain of that throughout the rest of her life. In the end we see that Travers has written *Mary Poppins* as a sort of autobiography, wanting still to honor her father and remember him well. I quickly felt some sense of divine activity in my urge to watch both films. The magic was palpable.

As I watched, I related to the young Travers and I swallowed hard - I felt sick with my judgments, sick with the pain of my life and the pain of the world. I related and I remembered; I cried and I cried. I wondered, *How much of my life has been wasted misjudging? How many times have I taken something at face-value, never slowing the mind and heart enough to see beyond appearance, into story and heart? How often have I missed the ending, misinterpreted a person's life entirely?*

My mind slowed for a second, and then raced on. *What makes it so hard to see past the seen? Haven't I, too, felt unknown, falsely accused, wrongfully labeled? Shouldn't I know better? Shouldn't I know, especially now, that everyone has a story?* That, yes, of course, *things aren't always what they seem.*

I watched and I listened and was enthralled with the whole film. I see Mr. Banks for the first time; I hear his story, and I know it. I see him in his pain and in his intentions and in his own mess and failures. I see him in his love and his humor; I see him through his daughter's eyes. I see, with certainty, myself in his daughter and him in me. I see their sadness and their life and I know: *things are not what they seem.*

Perhaps they seem empty or broken or disfigured beyond repair. Perhaps they seem pleasant or calm or more or less content. And perhaps, if you are like me, you are viewing it all, claiming what *seems*, through lenses of life-learned blame and numbness and distrust and fear. Lenses of assumptions and prejudices and scars deep within our subconscious. Maybe you have reached around and found nothing, given up in despair. But, perhaps - what if? - *things are not what they seem.*

What if we kept looking? Kept daring to believe in impossible somethings, magical risings from within? What if we took off our judgment-tainted glasses, peered deep into the mysteries before us, and found life - true and beautiful and satisfying? What if we laid our assumptions down, took our defenses off and demanded ourselves, with bare, trembling hands, to embrace the humanity and inherent worth of every soul around us? What if, in doing so, we found strength and magic and meaning beyond compare?

Writing Prompt: Write about a time you misjudged someone or something. When and how did you realize that your perceptions were off? What does the idea, *things are not what they seem*, mean for your life today?

BELOVED

You won't know how to explain that there is nothing nominal or lukewarm or indifferent about standing in this hurricane of questions every day and staring each one down until you've mustered all the bravery and fortitude and trust it takes to whisper just one of them out loud on the car ride home: "What if we made this up because we're afraid of death?"
Rachel Held Evans, *Searching For Sunday*

Last June, my husband and I decided to enjoy a rare evening together on our back porch in the warmth of a summer sunset. With drinks in hand, kids in bed and fresh air all around, it was hard not to relax. We sipped and reminisced and often fell into silence. My guard was down and I relished the peace of his presence. At one point in our conversation, we began talking about the Christian concept of a Savior. Having both strongly adhered to evangelical Christianity for decades, it was both a profound and deeply personal topic of conversation to dive into, and we did so with both great courage and deep longing.

After losing our son in 2010, my husband and I both went through our own tumultuous, unique spiritual journeys. Though many of the questions in our hearts were the same - *Why? God, where are you? How could a good God let this happen?* - we processed each in different time and with different outcomes. We had both stopped attending church and had largely torn off any religious labels we'd previously worn. I resorted often to isolation, living in the past and playing the devil's advocate. Daniel's drug of choice tended to be anger and skepticism. And yet, we found ourselves better able to empathize with others in their pain, more attuned and available to the needs around us, and resiliently positive about the family and future we were building.

At the time of our summer sunset conversation, it had been over three years since that defining loss, but the wound was still very fresh, and the questions were still endless. With that background heavy in our hearts, we tried to figure out if any of the old labels still fit. *Were we Christians? Were we "saved" and what did that even mean? What did we believe?*

I remember realizing for the first time that I no longer identified with the idea of needing a Savior to forgive my sins. I had slowly started walking into a space of self-acceptance, one which would later continue to flourish and grow, and I found no space there for the concept of a sinful nature and a Savior to redeem it. I remember confessing to my husband, *"I guess I don't understand what I need saved from? I've realized that we are all broken and messy and that* **it's okay***. I always wanted Jesus to help make me perfect, to present me as perfect before God. But, I'm okay with not being perfect now. I actually prefer myself this way, the messier, more content me. I accept me, questions and flaws and all. So - it's hard for me to say this out loud, but - Jesus as I have always understood him just seems irrelevant now. If I love me as I am, if I believe I'm actually good and enough at my core, what do I need a Savior to make me perfect for?"*

It was a hard confession to make and prompted more conversations and lots more introspection. I realized that this idea of being "inherently good" was taking root in my heart, in such strong opposition to all I'd been raised to believe. As I opened my heart more, began going to counseling, writing regularly and reading ravenously, I could no longer run from the constant theme of learning to love myself, of embracing authenticity and believing that I am imperfect and I am enough. The more I accepted myself, the more foreign the Savior concept became.

~:~

Recently, I wrote on my blog about false selves. And now it's come up in my reading again. And again. Impostors, glittering images, illusory selves, shadows. It feels like a divine message - *a warning?* I try to stand with open hands to what is being said, to give my heart over to the humbling act of learning.

A sentence jumps off the page at me as I read Benner's, *The Gift of Being Yourself*: *"We do not like what we see. It is uncomfortable - intolerable - to confront our true selves."* I physically squirm in my seat when I read the words, re-reading a time or two to make sure I haven't skipped a necessary negative that would alter the meaning of the sentence completely. But, no, the meaning doesn't change. The author seems to be claiming that seeing who we really are is painful, awful even. I resist this familiar judgment. I struggle to keep my hands open, rather than clenching them in staunch resistance.

Is the point that I am - at my truest, deepest self - awful, bad, flawed, broken? I ask myself. Is there truth anywhere in that? Is that even what this author is trying to communicate? Because I have breathed deep of this toxic message many, many times before and ultimately found it to be ruinous to my soul.

I read on and continue to find words that touch a wounded place within - God loving us despite our shortcomings, God humbling himself to meet us. Then these quotes by Thomas Merton appear, *"Surrender your poverty and acknowledge your nothingness to the Lord."* and, *"The reason we never enter into the deepest reality of our relationship with God is that we so seldom acknowledge our utter nothingness before him."* I feel that old piercing, that old posture of shame and worthlessness. So I resist, resist, resist.

I have to ask, *Am I "utter nothingness?" Am I so broken and flawed that I need the pity of Divinity, Who made me?* I struggle with these, sit back and physically unclench my hands to help my soul relax into the questions. I am no longer content with quick answers or defensive arguments. I want to press in, to learn, to live wholly.

I wonder, *Is it something false in me - wanting to be good, capable, right - that resists this "nothingness" so staunchly?* I try to look from all side, try giving myself room to be wrong. But I am soon pulled back to a place of self-love, of more than enough. *What if I have taken off the masks and have fallen in love with what is left? What if I have seen the true self and like her, accept her?* I question if even this is foolishness, to think that I have come so full-circle in knowing and loving my true self. It seems necessary to look back, to re-walk the journey of awakening I have been on of late.

And so I look back and see that in recent months I have learned - and have known deeper in my being for so much longer - that I have posed as the Capable One, hidden behind masks labeled Willing & Able, identified with adherence to rules and accomplishment of all I try. I've been Achiever, Believer, Faithful Friend & Follower. I am Doer. These are my false selves, my glittering images. They have let me live life pleasing others and accomplishing and hiding in my doing, rather than just being. I have resisted stopping - resisted giving up labels or resting in a moment just for pleasure. I have silenced questions, thwarted creativity, resisted change, always in pursuit of the accolades of doing.

Then, finally, I found myself incapacitated, incapable of continuing to hide behind all the doing. When life delivered me one blow after another of tragedy and chaos and confusion, it seemed to be a Divine bidding to stop and sit in silence. Even then, I didn't *have* to look or to listen. Even then, I didn't *want* to open my eyes to the reality of these false selves or to listen to the hard truths of my numbing and hiding. Many times I considered running away, hiding again, fleeing from all the uncertainty and possibility. But something inside wouldn't let me go back to the old ways, something inside urged me to sit in the darkness.

And in that darkness - in the loneliness and pain, in the confusion and uncertainty of that darkness - I finally started to see. It is as author Barbara Taylor Brown says in her book, *Learning to Walk in the Dark*:
> ...*the dark night is God's best gift to you, intended for your liberation. It's about freeing you from your ideas about God, your fears about God, your attachment to all the benefits you have been promised for believing in God, your devotion to spiritual practices that are supposed to make you feel closer to God, your dedication*

to doing and believing all the right things about God, your positive and negative evaluations of yourself as a believer in God, your tactics for manipulating God, and your sure cures for doubting God. All of these are substitutes for God.

There are depths in Brown's knowing that I have not yet reached, but I see the Light around the corner. I see truth beyond my performing or numbing or constant doing. I see a truer self, a *me* beneath the masks, awakening out of the nothingness that life's darkness is leading me through.

And as I grapple with this becoming and all the questions stirring within, I ask myself, *Who is this truer self that I claim to love? What lies beyond the masks, beyond the Doer? Who am I at my core, the she that writhes at the thought of being pitied in her "nothingness?"*

I answer with this: she is aware - aware that life is made up of grand dichotomies - of suffering and laughter, of deep grief and true joy, of the need to stand firm and the beauty of mystery. Aware that life is found in the *balance* of it all. She is awake to the truth that none are spared, that we are all human and thus in this great drama called life together. In *togetherness* we find meaning. She believes all are equal, all are welcome, all are beauty and creativity and inherent worth. She knows that life is messy, that things don't always go as planned and that often there are no answers to the aching questions within. She knows that embracing suffering is the key to intimacy - that feeling our feels and voicing the pain, even while embracing the joy, is the pathway to the fullest life lived. *That living life with hands and hearts wide open is the most courageous, gut-wrenching, meaningful existence of all.*

She believes in speaking all, letting light into the shadows and calling forth what wills to hide. She believes in connection - deep soul conversations between two beings of Divine creation, free from dogma or duty or dependence on defining life into blacks and whites. She believes in Gray. In Mystery. In Mist, that may only be seen in passing glimpses or subtle smells, but is Truth and Life nonetheless. She calls life a journey and is eager to live it learning and experiencing and taking it all in anew every day. She believes in growth and the constancy of change.

She is amazed at the miracle of children, and often in awe at the responsibility of raising such delicate spirits, and the potential to thwart such beauty and life. She wills to give and to serve, to know and be known. She thinks all are artists, with their own forms of expression. She thinks life can be mess and magic and mundane, *all at once.* She seeks to see the magic. She believes in forgiveness, including herself. She knows we are capable of the worst, but created for the best. She errs on the side of compassion, but is not immune to judgment or comparison, negativity or ungratefulness. She believes the root of Divine creation is goodness, is beauty, is truth and love and light. She seeks Truth and Love above all else.

Is she, then, my truest self? It seems almost vain to even ask this. And yet, in my gut I know this is the becoming that all the darkness and all the silence has led me to. Continues to lead me toward. But I know, too, that there are the impostors, the glittering images that grip and grapple and conceal this true self. That my masks are far too often the dominate realities of my existence, made alive by my fears, animated by my shame and insecurity. I know I must name the masks to know them, to be aware and live free of them. And so I look further into the darkness.

And I see this: The impostor is productive and capable and always saying *yes*. She is busy and distracted and always on the move. Appearance matters and perfection is preferred. She is haunted by a lurking sense of not being enough, not being lovable. She secretly fears nobody truly accepts her; she reads into canceled appointments and unresponsive friendships, and fears rejection. She is insecure in relationships, tired of always being the go-to-girl, desperate for a friend to be for her what she has been for so many. She sees past those right in front of her.

She searches for answers and holds on tightly to all the "*What ifs?*" She wants control and order, cleanliness and organization. She prefers the neatness of labels, despite the confusion and confinement they create. She feels the constant tension of Gray, and squirms to define herself into one side or the other. She counts the losses, tallies the suffering, remembers the pain. She loses heart in the shadows. She fears the "*next bad thing,*" awaits some impending doom.

She longs to be defined by her being, but cannot see life beyond doing. She is known as Do, and when she has tried to stop, she feels life and love have, too. She cannot fully relish the joy or give thanks for the good, for the pain and skepticism of life's losses simmer on the surface of her heart, creating a fog. She considers Mystery and concludes Unknowable and Unconcerned. She considers Mist and shrivels in despair. She craves acceptance and worth and belonging and love. She settles for half-feeling and hard-working.

~:~

I refill my coffee, pick Brenner's book back up, and soon come to this, "*Self-rejection is the greatest enemy of the spiritual life because it contradicts the sacred voice that calls us the "Beloved." Being the Beloved constitutes the core truth of our existence.*" My heart skips a beat, flutters at the lightness and life of these words. This resonates as deep truth to me, for it is the essence of so much of my recent awakening.

But I am confused. A link is missing and I ask out loud, *Is this the same author?!* I cannot understand how the principle of my nothingness and the core of my Beloved-ness can coexist. I ask, *How is the Beloved juxtaposed beside the Damned? How do I embrace myself as Beloved - the truest essence of my being as good - and still find the need for Divine compassion? If I am enough, even Beloved, what is forgiveness for? And why the need to lose myself, to become nothing, to die that He might live? What if* **I** *want to live?*

I see this is the crucial point for me: to be loved as I am. To be welcomed, flaws and all, not with pity or grace for all I don't deserve, but with a love compelled by my inherent value. I want to be accepted because I am beauty. I want to be known because I am worth. I want to be affirmed in goodness and embraced in wholeness.

In my masked days, this embracing love was the furthest thing from my daily experiences. Instead, I knew a self-rejection that couldn't find more than a fairly capable mind and somewhat shapely shoulders in all of my being to admire. I functioned in a state of constant self-hate, repeating prayers of repentance day in and day out, journaling daily about my unworthiness and impossible shortcomings, thanking the skies above for looking on such a lowly one as me. I pleaded for Divine help, despaired in my never enoughs, strived to be more.

I dieted, made myself vomit and exercised obsessively. I sucked in and covered up and cried myself to sleep, reaching for a beauty that was always an arm's length away. I worked two jobs and earned straight A's and paid for college, exhausted and empty at the end of most days, motivated by a desperation to achieve, to please, to do it all "right." I skimped on sleep and skipped fun altogether, rushing through my days in a frenzied state of *Try Harder*. I sliced or seared or stuffed myself with pills in desperation and futility and hopelessness.

Never in all those days of striving and doing, of repenting and praying, did I experience any meaningful sense of being truly, inherently valuable. Not until the darkness closed in around me and I chose to sit with myself in silence, did I start to awaken to the beauty of *me*.

And now, today, as I become acquainted with self-acceptance, my soul has sighed deeply with relief. I have seen the "weaknesses" and have called them Enough. I have looked straight at the mess and known I am more. I have practiced liberation from *their* words and freedom from *their* judgment. I have set boundaries and have spoken my truth. I have embraced Mystery and felt alive in a profound way. I have marveled at creation - at sunsets and centipedes and self.

In light of all of this, I sit with nothingness in one hand and Beloved-ness in the other, baffled. I follow this line of questioning next: *Where is God in self-acceptance? Where is Divine Love in the midst of self-love? Is this, too, a matter of balance? Is there a full embracing and acceptance of self, and a full embracing of Divine forgiveness and compassion? A need for both?*

As if to confirm this mystery of *and*, I read on and find the following:

> "Hatred of the impostor is actually self-hatred. The impostor and I constitute one person. Contempt for the false self gives vent to hostility, which manifests itself as general irritability - an irritation at the same faults in others that we hate in ourselves. Self-hatred always results in some form of self-destructive behavior. Accepting the reality of our sinfulness means accepting our authentic self."

And though the picture is still blurry, I sense that this is, in fact, the missing link, the bridge that is built on *and*. That somewhere in this acceptance of my true self, there must also be acceptance of the impostors. That perhaps all of the writing on nothingness and poverty and Divine pity speaks to this call to also accept the false self as indivisibly, eternally part of me. An embracing of the reality that though my truest self is indeed beauty and beloved and goodness and kindness, that my false self, too, is me, even if to a far lesser degree.

The impostor is the insecure me, the wounded me, the me that wants to hide and perform and put up a front to survive. The me that finds fault and puffs up and frenzies on. And though I yearn to disown the impostor completely, I cannot deny that she is still part of me. I cannot run from the fact that it is a battle to live out my truest self, to daily live freely and creatively and kindly, to be fully *her*.

Perhaps it is this - the choice between living out the true self or the false selves - that makes possible the embracing of both self-love and Divine forgiveness. Perhaps it is free will, the profound privilege and responsibility of choice, that lends itself so necessarily to *and*. Perhaps I do not have to stoop back down to the self-hatred of inherent evil that once consumed me to accept that freedom means I am capable of all.

I am good, but capable of evil.
I am truth, but capable of lies.
I am beautiful, but capable of mess.
I am courage, but capable of cowardice.
I am kindness and creativity, but capable of cruelty and apathy.
I am empathy and compassion, but capable of criticism and selfishness.

If I am honest, I am still, in all my awakening and becoming and knowing of my truer self, often the impostor. *Far too often.* Not because it is ultimately who I am, but because I have a choice. Freedom with a price. The false and the true co-dwelling.

Could it be that Jesus forgives, not who I am, *but what I am capable of?* Could it be that Divine compassion speaks not to my essence, my truest self, but to the impostor that I often hide behind? Could it be that I AM speaks to who I am? Calls me to Himself to guide and encourage and empower me to choose the *I am* in me? To live out my truest self? Is it, in fact, Divine Love orchestrating my walk into self-love?

And then I read, *"Being the beloved is our identity, the core of our existence. It is not merely a lofty thought, an inspiring idea, or one name among many. It is the name by which God knows us and the way He relates to us. ... "Who am I?" asked Merton, and he responded, "I am one loved by Christ."*

Writing Prompt: If someone asked who your truest self is - *who you are at your core, what you believe and know with all your heart* - what would you answer? How does this differ from the person you are on a daily basis? What impostors can you name, and what would it mean to love both the true & false you?

WEIGHT

Slowly I began to trust the solitary voice in me that said that standing still meant forward progress, that letting life happen rather than striving to make it happen allowed life to unfold with even more beauty and potential, that facing pain wasn't nearly so terrible as avoiding it.
Sue Monk Kidd, *When the Heart Waits*

When I was ten, my family owned an old white Chevy station wagon, complete with wood paneling, brown leather throughout and seats that flipped up in the back to face each other. My siblings and I loved that station wagon, and always called *dibs* on getting to sit in the "way back." That meant both being out of hearing distance from my mother and face-to-face with one another: friends and accomplices. We loaded up, my three sisters and I - plus the extra five or so kids that my mom babysat on a regular basis - during a time before car seats or booster seats, when it was acceptable to sardine kiddos all in a row, strapped two per seatbelt.

My mother has always been frugal and holds tightly, to this day, to a smorgasbord of rules and old wives' tales on how to conserve money. She was a master at stretching our grocery budget in order to feed our family of seven and the extra kids she watched on *half* of what most people needed. Of course, this meant a lot of bologna sandwiches and Kool-Aid, but it was a feat I still respect today.

One of her more infamous rules was to never, unless absolutely necessary, use air conditioning. And for my mother, what constituted *absolutely necessary* was a matter of pure torture to most. This rule felt especially cruel in the middle of Georgia summers, mashed side-by-side with a half dozen other wriggly kids on leather seats, in ninety-plus degree heat, heading to swim team practice. My mother insisted on rolling windows down rather than wasting extra gas by using the air conditioning. We all writhed and whined at every stoplight when the breeze died down, sticky legs and sweaty backs beckoning the wind to blow again. I was always skeptical about how much gas was actually being saved and horrified when we inevitably arrived at our destination with rosy cheeks and wet rear-ends.

It was in that old white station wagon, sardined alongside my sisters, that I first became truly aware of my body. I remember sitting down on those sticky, hot leather seats one day and watching with horror as my thighs spread into what seemed like a never-ending mass of flesh. I vividly recall lifting and lowering my legs over and over, verifying the atrocity of thighs that were so full *they now spread.*

Now, at the time, I was a very lean, active ten-year-old. If you look at pictures of me, you'd see nothing but a slender, sun-kissed, beautiful little girl. I did well in swim team, was admired by the boys and was generally a self-confident child. But becoming aware of my thighs - those sweaty, spreading thighs - would be the first step toward *years* of a deteriorating body image.

Not too long after the thigh-spread incident, I discovered that my mom had a bottle of pills intended to help you get skinnier. It seemed like a simple, obvious answer to the growing doom I felt about my body, and so I soon started stealing those pills and taking them on a regular basis. They didn't seem to have any effect on my body, at least nothing that was startlingly obvious. But they had a profound impact on me emotionally. They taught me that it was normal to hate my body, and that there was a whole world out there ready and willing to help me fix all the unpleasant parts of me.

My addiction to dieting thus began in fifth grade.

I became increasingly aware of the eating habits of those around me, especially of my peers and my mother. In middle school, I learned that I could manipulate food to try to get the body I wanted, and I learned, too, that I wasn't the only one who hated what she saw in the mirror. I realized that I was now a part of the masses, and, both with insecurity and a feeling of belonging, I increased my attention to dieting and exercising.

I was a typical young tween: I would have rather died than let someone of the opposite sex see me eat. That meant by and large skipping lunch, or at the most eating a bag of Fun Yuns. It meant constantly lying about being hungry, sucking in my waistline at least 70% of the day and denying the fully-human experience of needing something to eat every few hours. All this, too, was done with a mixed sense of shame and camaraderie.

In addition to my increasing awareness of body and dieting, puberty came plowing through like a steam engine, adding curves to my hips and large mounds to my chest. I was in a size C-cup bra by seventh grade, and frequently mistaken to be several years older than my actual age. I was infatuated with the opposite sex and craved the attention they gave, which was largely positive and frequent. I learned that my body was not only something that I could control, *but something I could use to control others.*

In eighth grade, I competed on a winter YMCA swim team, a spring track and field team at my middle school, and then a summer country club swim team. That meant that for nearly a year straight, I attended at least an hour of physically demanding practices all week, and then competed all day on Saturdays. Somehow, despite all the exertion, I managed to limit my food intake, often to just a bowl of cereal in the morning and a hot dog or bagel after school. Because I had read somewhere that mustard helped increase one's metabolism, I allowed myself a heaping squirt of mustard with my hot dog or bagel. But that was it, for many days of my eighth grade year.

But despite these extreme measures, my body continued to grow and change - and I continued to feel helpless and increasingly despondent about what I saw in the mirror. It seemed that no matter how much effort I put forth, no matter how much I limited what I ate or how extensively I exercised, my body would not respond in the ways I wanted it to. I had no idea that the growth and change I was experiencing was completely normal and healthy, and also absolutely no perspective that I was actually a beautiful, fit young girl. All I saw was flesh and fat and ever-increasing imperfections.

In high school, I started to realize that I was stuck on a roller coaster of dieting and hating my body. I used to pray every night, sucking in as far as I could and squeezing my stomach tight, *"Go away fat. Go away fat,"* right after praying that my father would stop drinking and my friends would come to church with me. I was horrified and exasperated every year, when, despite all my efforts, I would need to buy larger sizes when it came time to go school shopping again. Growth meant nothing to me except failure. It was evidence that I hadn't done enough, that *I* wasn't enough, *that my own body rejected me.*

After reading an article in some teen magazine, I decided to become a vegetarian, in hopes that this would finally solve all my body woes. I fantasized about being a slim, confident, healthy woman, carefree and running wild in a bathing suit. I focused on eating fruits and vegetables, but struggled with never feeling full. I enjoyed the sense of control I felt over what was going into my body, but, still, was disappointed that I didn't lose weight. My bout of vegetarianism lasted through my junior year of high school, when a mission trip to India would require me to consume whatever was put on the plate in front me, including meat. It turned out my end with vegetarianism didn't matter anyways, because in my two years of refusing meat, I had only *gained* a few more pounds.

I continued to be active throughout high school: running track, competing in swim team and cheerleading both during football and basketball seasons. I also continued to diet, continued to grow, and continued to hate the body I had to live in. It was an endless cycle of effort, failure and self-rejection. I could never manage to gain enough perspective to see beauty in myself, let alone accept to my body and let go of the fight for someone slimmer.

Following my senior year of high school, I attended a yearlong Christian leadership internship in Texas. The program focused on the whole body, meaning that exercise and good health were a requirement. Although I had made the decision to attend for largely religious reasons, I was very drawn to the idea of a regular exercise regime and health as a Christian priority.

I left for Texas, having every intention of *finally* losing all the unwanted pounds and getting the fit, lean body I'd always dreamed of. I also yearned for the days that I could look in the mirror and like what I saw. I hoped that this would be the place to reach both goals.

But again, despite rising at 5:30 every morning to train for a 5K and exercising at least an hour a day, I ended up gaining ten pounds in my first four months in Texas. *Yes, ten pounds in four months* - by far my largest weight gain in such a short amount of time to-date. When I returned home for Christmas break, close to my nineteenth birthday and now a size ten, I remember overhearing my mother and uncle late one evening talking about my weight. It took my breath away to hear a topic that carried so much shame and stigma for me spoken of *out loud*. I was horrified to hear their concerns actually voiced.

I cried and cried that night, asking myself and God, *What's wrong with me?* I had spent the last eight years working and starving and trying so hard, only to grow and grow and grow. Extreme caloric restrictions hadn't helped, crazy fad diets of only cabbage soup or mustard bagels weren't the answer, and exercise only made me hungrier. I felt my body had betrayed me and now my failure was obvious, a topic of late-night, hushed-voice conversations.

To add to the trauma of overhearing that conversation, I was also struggling with my mother's recent weight loss success. While I had spiraled further out of control, she had finally found her dieting fit. After all sorts of pills and plans, my mother landed on the protein-based Atkins diet and lost a significant amount of weight, quickly. So much, that when I returned for Christmas break, she was now smaller than me. *Significantly smaller.* I couldn't bear the thought of not being able to squeeze into my own mother's jeans. I returned to Texas, despondent and desperate.

I decided to give dieting one last go and stuck feverishly to the Atkins diet that had worked so well for my mom. After over a month, though, I still hadn't lost any weight. I was so incensed and confused, I started checking the seasoning salt I'd been using on my morning eggs to see if it was secretly laced with sugar, and thus the cause of all those pounds still holding on. I could not understand why my body wasn't responding, why it wouldn't just listen to my constant pleas to *please shrink.* I was furious with my body for rejecting me. I gave Atkins one more month and upped my exercise routine.

Still nothing.

My body image, by this point, had become a frequent point of conversation between God and I. I prayed about my desire to be thinner, my exhaustion with the dieting roller coaster, my hate at what I saw in the mirror. I mostly asked for help to shed the unwanted weight, but I also started asking for help to accept what I'd been given. I could see that with each year of effort and self-rejection, I only grew larger. The body I had and hated at twelve would become the body that I wanted and strived for at fourteen. The body I had and hated at fourteen would become the body I wanted and strived for at sixteen. And so on.

When the Atkins diet failed, on my nineteenth birthday, I gave up on my body and decided I was meant to be fat and unfulfilled forever. I gave in to all the suppressed appetites and sadness and gained another twenty pounds in the next six months. I was furious at how quickly my body would take on weight, after having refused for years to let go of it. But, by then, I was largely resigned to being an unhappy, overweight woman. I returned home from Texas a full, round, miserable size 14.

~:~

Hating the way you look, despising the body that you wake up to every morning and that carries you day in and day out, is an absolutely exhausting existence. I think of all the years of energy and focus I gave to trying to shrink my body and mold it into something it wasn't. I think of all the tears, all the self-conscious glances over my shoulder and all the misery of never, ever feeling beautiful enough. I think of that feeling of defeat, experienced over and over again, that message that I would always hate my body, that I was not capable of change, that this was just a woman's lot in life.

I see pictures of myself at ten and twelve and fourteen and want to wrap her in my arms and tell her how beautiful she is. Tell her how normal growth is, that her body was meant to change and that it was not because of anything she did wrong. I would beg her to look through my eyes, will her to see herself in a different light, a more truthful light. I would ask her to repeat after me, *"I am lovely. I am enough."* Over and over and over again until it sunk far enough into her core that all the self-hate began to crack.

~:~

While at my heaviest weight, I traveled to Germany for a semester. I lived with a lovely group of young German women, who were eccentric and diverse and absolutely enchanting. Two were from the former East and two from the former West. One was of German-Korean decent and one spoke six languages fluently. They were cultured and witty and wonderful companions.

At some point during my visit, in between bites of fresh rolls and creamy brie, one of my roommates, Ulie, inquired about my weight. I was the heaviest of the group and deeply insecure about my weight. Ulie was very slender, with gorgeous curly brown hair that flowed down to her waist. She had flawless, delicate peach skin and an enormous smile. She was kind in her approach, but also not at all tip-toeing like an American would be with the subject. She asked, in her direct German way, *"Have you always been this heavy? Tell me about your weight."*

Other than the evening I had overheard my mother and uncle discussing my weight, my body had always been a topic I held closely, in a corner of privacy and silence. I was so consumed with shame over my body that I dared not open my mouth and hoped that somehow my silence would keep others from noticing the problem at all. It was a tactic I had learned along the way, avoiding the hard things, muting the pain. It was better not to speak.

But Ulie didn't seem to carry any of these same stigmas and in her gentle, matter-of-fact questioning, I found just the space I needed to finally speak about my body. In the course of our conversation, I was able to both acknowledge how out-of-balance my eating had become, how unhappy I was with my body and also how defeated I felt to ever experiencing change. Ulie shared of her own weight struggles, confessed that just years earlier she had been overweight and in her own spiral of self-hate. It was impossible to imagine this beautiful, intelligent woman before me - *perfect skin, perfect body, perfect hair* - ever having thought negatively about herself. The distortion of our body-hating finally sunk in to me that day.

Ulie asked if she could pray for me, pray that God would help me get off the roller coaster. She said this sort of prayer had been a significant turning point in her own journey toward self-acceptance. I agreed, hesitatingly and skeptically. Yet as I listened to Ulie pray, I realized that all the pain and shame I'd carried about my weight, for at least a decade, was already shrinking. Just from having been spoken and owned, just from having been voiced out loud and embraced with love and tenderness, I felt the heaviness of the shame, the bottling up of this *"deep, dark secret,"* losing its grip. I felt physically and emotionally lighter and freer that very day.

There was something significant that broke that night, that loosened or cracked just enough to allow me to wriggle off the roller coaster *slowly but surely*. Changes in my body were not at all instantaneous, and frankly, my body image itself was slow to change, too. But shortly after that conversation with Ulie, nearing my twenty-first birthday, I vowed to disown dieting and extreme exercise regimes for the first time since fifth grade. I decided, finally, to stop focusing on my body or my weight, to stop setting goals or making resolutions or imagining life when I could finally fit into that old pair of jeans. It wasn't that I could say I liked what I saw, I was just so ready to stop scrutinizing and hating myself so much.

In hindsight, I can see that the decision to release my grip on my body, to stop trying to control and manufacture myself into a certain image, was both extremely courageous and completely miraculous. Perhaps it is like an alcoholic deciding one day never to take a drink again, while still living in the same town, driving past that same bar. I was faced constantly with the reality of needing to eat and having to look at myself in the mirror, meals three times a day, grocery shopping, getting dressed every morning. Food and weight and clothes fitting, or not, were still a part of every other moment. Yet somehow, the decision to turn from this obsession, to release this addiction, actually stuck. And for me, after so many years of living with my body on the throne of judgment, front-and-center, day-in-and-day-out, *it was a miracle.*

I started working two full-time jobs and started attending full-time classes at The Ohio State University that Spring. I was living on my own for the first time, trying to pay the bills and clean the house and do my laundry in between insane work and school schedules. All of this new responsibility lead to such a jam-packed schedule that I lost an incredible amount of weight. Almost thirty pounds in a year, in fact.

Ironic, don't you think?

For the first time in my life, I experienced the inconceivable: food was not playing center stage in my day. In fact, sometimes it played such a small role that I would often forget to eat altogether, which was something I used to think skinny girls made up just to show off. I marveled, a bit begrudgingly I admit, when I realized several months after that initial decision to stop focusing on my diet and hating my body, that I was down to size 8 jeans *after not having exercised or dieted at all.*

~:~

This is my story, my journey of trying to control and manipulate and obtain an elusive weight, then finally giving up, letting go, walking courageously away from the chains of self-hate. In no way do I think this is a model of healthy, balanced living or that busyness is a formula those still on the roller coaster should use as their next weight loss trick. But it was such a miracle that I could function without food and my weight as the primary concern, that this kind of imbalance was exactly where *I* needed to be.

I stayed in that place for a couple of years, meeting my husband during that season of life and finding a whole new level of acceptance and appreciation for my body through him. Eventually I would introduce structured exercise back into my life, but never as a consistent discipline or a means to getting into a certain pair of jeans. I would "diet" again, eight years later, after the birth of my second child. But this time it was temporarily monitoring daily intake with a whole different frame of mind and I would feel freedom still, despite the structure. I had found a place of self-worth that was not tied to my appearance.

I think of all those years of body-loathing and I still cringe at how much I took for granted. I weep for the child, the young girl, that felt so much sadness and despair and betrayal at something that was such a natural, biological inevitability: *Growth.* I recoil at the realization of all the beauty and health that I had, and my inability to *see* it. But I marvel, too, at the journey. *I am in awe of daily living without loathing.* Of love and admiration for this sagging, pocked, mother-of-two body of mine. And I am forever thankful for beauty and the ability, finally, to see it.

Writing Prompt: How would you describe your relationship with your body? Describe any evolution in your body-image that you have experienced over the years? What would you say to your younger self if you saw her today?

DO

There's a reason they call God a presence - because God is right here, right now. In the present is the only place to find Him, and now is the only time.

Elizabeth Gilbert, *Eat, Pray, Love*

My mind is racing with these questions, noisy echoes of too-busy days - days unsatisfied, frenzied with trying, ending with emptiness, guilt, fatigue. I lie awake at night and ask myself:

Why am I so distracted all the time? Why do I feel so compelled to keep all the plates spinning and to respond to the incessant to-do lists? Why does productivity matter to me so much, and why do I always say "yes?" Why, why is it so hard to stop?

I torture myself with moments passed, affections missed, smiles unacknowledged. I toss and turn, too guilty to sleep, too exhausted to answer my own questions. I am caught in a web of effort, of controlling and doing, of longing and loving. I search for an answer, then, well past midnight, *I finally fall asleep.*

~:~

I have been extremely distracted lately. And this state of being distracted, well, *it's distracting.* I don't think it's likely that anything new is distracting me, just that I'm waking up to all the noise that's been there all along. I sit down to play baby dolls with my two-year-old daughter and almost instantly my mind wanders to the bow tie orders I need to be filling and the fabric that needs ordered and the emails that need sent, and I'm down a mile-long list of business to-do's before I realize she is still sitting there, waiting with her baby doll. It's excruciating for a moment, but my wheels are spinning too fast to stay in one emotion for long.

Later on, I sit with my son to build trains and again, like second nature, my mind is racing with writing prompts and analogies I want to remember and books I need to read and others I forgot to return and fines that need paid and the spinning mental to-do list consumes me all over again. I look tiredly back at my son, happily driving his train around the track we've started. I decide to give myself ten minutes to send a couple emails and get all the laundry gathered, hoping that by checking off a couple of the to-do's, I will again be able to focus and breathe.

I excuse myself from the kids, pleading with them to play kindly with each other while I'm gone. I send the emails, but am distracted by the mess of the office and in the midst of sorting piles and picking up crayons, I hear crying and screaming from the basement. I find both children sobbing at the bottom of the steps, one having been hit by a sword and the other bitten in retaliation. I fume at them for not being able to play together for ten minutes while mama gets some work done. I situate them on the couch with a cup of raisins and a show, then resume my sorting and cleaning and, *after checking emails again,* gather the laundry.

By this time, the kids are frantic for my attention and I'm consumed with guilt for all the distraction, stressed even more by the endless list of to-do's. My "ten minute" break has turned into a half hour of frenzied doing, and I plead with myself to just slow down and let my focus rest entirely on these two beautiful children. I drop the laundry basket at the top of the stairs, straighten a few cushions on my way back, then plop down beside warm, welcoming bodies.

I'm able to breathe into some time with the kids, cuddle with them while reading books and sit down for lunch together. My mind flitters off here and there throughout our cuddles and conversations, but mostly I'm present and warding off the Do Demon with the hopes of productive nap time hours, quickly approaching. We chitter-chatter and cleanup from lunch and I have this urgent sense of wanting to freeze time, to savor these moments forever. For a moment I am caught up in what really matters.

Then, I race to lay the kids down for naps - dreading the day I won't have those hours to slash my to-do lists in half - and run downstairs, dashing from item to item, responding to more emails, finally throwing in that load of laundry, cleaning the kitchen, *timing my every step*. I check in with my list, check the clock for the hundredth time, allow myself a four minute shower, respond to more emails, numb with a scan of the news feed, then race back downstairs to switch the laundry. Multiple times, I realize my heart is racing from trying to squeeze four hours into an hour and a half. I try to take deep breaths, to think of a better way. I add *"exercise"* and *"write"* to my to-do list as I race upstairs to gather too-soon woken children.

The day continues on, with laundry to fold and floors to sweep, groceries to buy and errands to run, food to cook and kids to love. We stop by the park for a mental breather, and I'm able to relax again, briefly, and breathe deep when we look eye-to-eye. But all too soon my mind races and in my frenzy, I find myself repeating tasks, over-checking emails, numbing to news feeds and staring past the people I love the most. By the end of the day, I'm exhausted, guilty, frustrated and still have a few more to-do's to finish up before I can collapse into bed. I end with a pending list on my desk and set my alarm for earlier the next day. *Maybe an earlier start will help?*

~:~

I have long, long been a juggler of many plates. I've proudly received the comment, *"just don't know how you do it all!"* hundreds of times and have breathed deeply of my ability to stretch the limits of a tight schedule and check off every last to-do on my list. I have also found room to check off others' to-do lists, being the go-to-girl for hosting baby showers and birthday parties and babysitting and volunteering for some project or another. My *yes's* have outweighed my *no's* a million to one, while I meticulously schedule each minute and write endless to-do lists.

When my husband and I met and married in 2005, I was working a 30 hour a week job, volunteering at least 10 hours a week with our church's college ministry, keeping up a packed social calendar and finishing out my senior year at The Ohio State University, where I petitioned every quarter for permission to take above the maximum allowable credit hours. I was paying my way through school - refusing to take on any debt - living on my own and planning a wedding. I literally ran (or sped) from one responsibility to the next, never saying "*no*" to a new opportunity to serve. Rather, I volunteered myself - my time and energy and talents - constantly, to family and friends and any reasonably needy cause. When people would ask, "*Are you sure you have time for that?*" I would proudly answer, "*Oh, yeah, I really thrive best under pressure. It's no problem at all!*"

And so the responsibilities would pile on and the multi-tasking would become incessant. Somehow, I'd manage to keep all the plates spinning, with astonishing success, and would marvel with others at my ability to take on so much. I didn't realize at the time that all the doing was morphing into a total identity, an addiction of being. I didn't realize that I was losing the ability to *just be*.

My husband has always been my biggest fan, and in those early years of marriage, I remember how impressed he was with how much I could handle and how thoughtful I was about using my time intentionally. I lived and breathed by an "*Intentional Time Use*" mantra. I was obsessed with productivity and using every second of my day to check something off my to-do list, which fortunately included relationships and ministry and volunteering. But instead of endless evenings of laughter or sharing, my friendships were grown during volunteer hours or while doing the laundry or over a ministry planning meeting. I had a hard time allowing myself to stop and saw little value in activities purely intended for pleasure. Life was being shared, but largely because we were all rushing from one activity to the next, together. In hindsight, many of my relationships were built on shared activity and convenience rather than commitment and depth. It's a subtle nuance that I would later find makes all the difference in the world.

~:~

Some of my earliest memories are defined around achieving and doing, which have continued to carry me, ensnaring me, defining me. Is it this need to be all, do all, never say "*no,*" that creates all the noise? Am I compelled toward an illusory standard, reaching in all directions for unobtainable control and perfection, *worth in the wrong places*? Is it the Do Demon, calling to me from every corner and crevice, craving my attention, resulting in my distraction?

I recently read Ann Voskamp's book, *One Thousand Gifts,* a beautifully written memoir of her personal quest to find meaning and hope and answers in this far-too messy world. She dives deeply into a practice of gratitude, and there finds much of what she's looking for. Beyond the beautiful language, what I love most about Voskamp's book is her honest reflection of the ebbs and flows of spirit that are so present in any true soul journey: One day you're living and loving through your fullest, freest, truest self and the next, you can't see past your own nose. You're yelling at the kids and wiping up mess and wondering why you're even alive.

On one such ebbing day, Voskamp writes, *"I speak it to God: I don't really want more time: I just want enough time. Time to breathe deep and time to see real and time to laugh long, time to give You glory and rest deep and sing joy and just enough time in a day not to feel hounded, pressed, driven, or wild to get it all done - yesterday."*

I so relate.

Hasn't that been my soul's cry? The source of all my recent angst? I'm so angry and frustrated with all the distraction, all the incessant noise, because I'm so desperate to be here, *right here, right now.* To slow down and savor this present time. To breathe into the second I'm currently living. To experience life *in time*, not a to-do list behind or a scrapbook later. I want to experience this moment of life, **in this moment of my life.**

And yet, something in me squirms and squeals, *"This moment isn't enough."* Oh, that fatal word, *enough.* It haunts me again and I feel my uneasiness at its judgment. I let *enough* sink in, press into the discomfort of it and listen to the Do Demon speak her truth. She says, *"It's not enough to have a messy floor and piles of laundry and counters that need wiped off. Maybe you can let it slide for a moment, maybe even a day, but it will still be there tomorrow. Just do it now. And you have to respond to every email you get - do you want people to think you are rude or unprofessional? Don't you want people to like you, to respect you? Who has time to rest, we have bills to pay and a home to maintain. If you don't do it, who will? Keep going, keep working, keep pushing through. It's up to you."*

And then I hear it, the lie I have always, always believed, *"You'll feel better once you get it all done."* I hear it and I know it's a lie. I have lived and breathed, *"Do it now"* and it has *not* satisfied. I have not felt better with everything checked off, because the lists just fill up all over again. There's always more to do. Checking off my to-do list may bring a temporary high, *but doing has not been the cure.*

I sit longer and listen. Enough...enough...enough. *Why wouldn't this moment be enough?* Because I'm scared it will let me down. I'm scared if I don't plan the next moment, it will bring disappointment or pain or loss instead. Afraid that if I don't control everything, keep all the plates spinning, stay in motion, my whole world will fall apart. I'll find myself flat, face down. *Right now* is so vulnerable, it is gone so fast. I'm scared of losing now, afraid of all the now's being lost into one big meaningless life. It is fear and pain and self-protection. I am afraid of now, desperate for some semblance of control, distracted by the lessers.

Voskamp later writes, *"I have lived the runner, panting ahead in worry, pounding back in regrets, terrified to live in the present, because here-time asks me to do the hardest thing of all: just open wide and receive."* Yes, this is me. The vulnerable twinge of being open wide in this very moment and the self-protective urge to run around controlling and planning and doing in distraction.

Yet life still ticks on, second by second, steady and sure. And haven't I known that well? Haven't I known that all my planning and doing doesn't control today, doesn't deliver a better tomorrow? Broken friendships, dead dreams, deep disappointments and childhood wounds; baby ripped out of my arms and beautiful friend smashed into the grave? Haven't I tasted, with bitterness and tears, that life and mess and loss will happen, regardless of how much I distract against it? Haven't I stood waving goodbye, all the lists still in my pocket, all the right boxes checked off again and again, and known it is not up to me? That all my doing didn't save her or bring him back? That all my effort didn't earn loyalty or love or freedom from loss?

I see with wide-eyes the mastery of Do to deceive and distract, to lead me into endless days of effort with promises of life *tomorrow* - a tomorrow that never comes. I see, today, how easily I could wrestle with my recent distractions and get frustrated with feeling like I'm not focusing on my kids enough or my business enough or my husband enough or even myself enough. I could make a plan, write a list, read a book, get to work. And it might work, and things might get better. But it's more likely that I'd be right back here, frustrated and guilty and distracted all over again - tomorrow, next week, next month - because all the lists and all the doing just didn't cut it. Because the doing promises achievement, but delivers anxiety; the doing promises satisfaction, but delivers futility.

The soul's journey is a constant ebbing and flowing - embracing truth, sliding into imbalance, flowing back into life. Today, I try to reacquaint myself with balance, with *just enough*. I accept my own limitations. I still plan and prioritize, but I allow for change, for *"not enough"* to be more than enough, for *"half-done"* to be just fine. I call the lies for what they are, the empty promises by name. I breathe deeper and, one moment at a time, try to choose Be over Do. With clenched teeth, I practice opening wide and receiving *now*.

Writing Prompt: Explore the concepts of *"mindfulness"* and *"presence"* in your life - past and present. What is your relationship with Do? What is your relationship with Be?

ANATOMY

Instead of telling our vulnerable stories, we seek safety in abstractions, speaking to each other about our opinions, ideas, and beliefs rather than about our lives.
Parker Palmer, *A Hidden Wholeness*

"*Butt penis! Butt penis! Butt penis!*" This, the sing-songy chant of my three-year-old son on our way home from a family gathering, hardly registered to me as abnormal. Until his two-year-old sister shrilled, "*Ky stop! Mama, Ky's being yucky!*" my mama brain had taken the song in stride as the creative expression of a rambunctious toddler boy. "*Ok, Kyler. That's enough. Let's sing about something else.*" My usual ploy of redirection calmed and cured immediately in this instance.

~:~

As with many young girls of my generation, I grew up fully ashamed of anatomically correct terminology for what we, with hushed voices, learned to call "*my private parts.*" It seemed they were so private, they carried a magical stigma of silence, never to be spoken of directly. I was of the line that softens natural bodily functions by using demure words like "*tinkle*" and "*number 2.*" Anything more direct was considered crass, a bad word. Like whining in disbelief, "*Mommy, she just said a bad word!!*" after hearing a sibling say *"poop."* We were expected to be polite and discreet, especially when it came to the female body.

As best as I can remember, like many girls, my three sisters and I were never taught a specific word for our vaginas. Rather, everything in that region was called *"my bottom."* If there was a replacement term, it has since faded from my memory. What has stuck is the shock of hearing the word *vagina* first spoken out loud, repeatedly, in my 7th grade health class. And if *vagina* spewing from the mouth of my handsome health teacher was not bad enough, hearing my crush's genitalia spoken of with words like *penis* and *scrotum* (rather than *"pee-tail,"* which is all I had ever heard a penis referred to at that point) caused my face to flush and my blood pressure to spike.

Every utterance of these direct terms was accompanied by the usual adolescent snickering. You could tell the few students who had heard such words spoken with more directness and regularity by the way they remained blank-faced, as though we were in history class hearing the upteenth lecture on Abraham Lincoln's assassination. I envied their calm, their ability to hear these words and process them as just another science lesson. But that wasn't my reality. For most of us, we lowered our heads, fiddled with scraps of paper and pencils, felt the heat in our cheeks burning hot. I left each day with a mixed sense of shame, intrigue and complete confusion.

The following year, in eighth grade, I discovered spots of blood in my underwear (at the time, we still politely called our underwear *"panties,"* like genteel southern belles who only ever wore lace and white). Thankfully, I had been made aware of this phenomenon by that scandalous 7th grade health class and by the gossip-filled, panic-inducing public gathering place, also known as the middle school cafeteria.

When the red specks appeared, however, I could not have been more surprised, or more dismayed. Every time I had a period, it felt like a curse to be endured, a foulness to be concealed. I knew how to beautify the act of urination and soften the references to my female parts, but how could I speak with discretion about a gaping wound dripping hot and red from between my legs? And so I didn't. *Ever.*

For years, I survived on stolen tampons and wads of toilet paper, until I finally worked up the courage to use my own money to go purchase feminine products myself. The first time I dared such an act, rather than being a liberating step in my feminine journey, I proceeded with great shame and secrecy. I hid the tampons under a pile of other items and made sure to turn away from the cashier when she finally unearthed the box. As she scanned them, *swords of knowing,* my face flushed - just like that health class several years back - at what seemed to be an earth-shattering beep, announcing, *"Attention, customers. This girl bleeds!"* I was horrified and quick-stepped my way to the car, tying my bag in tight knots along the way and vowing never to be so publicly known again.

Much later, in my thirties, I would speak to high school friends who told of their own struggle with shame during those years. Beyond the usual body image obsessions and the adolescent turmoil of fitting in, many of us were also carrying the weight of this dark secret: *we were female.* We were concealing our menstrual cycles, often from one another, but most certainly from our parents. We had no language for the becoming we were experiencing and thus, we retreated in secrecy and silence. It wasn't that anybody ever spoke with such negativity about our bodies or our menstruations, is was just that nobody ever spoke. And so neither did we.

At the same time that all this concealing and silencing of our feminine becoming was imploding within, we were also faced with growing sexual attractions. I had my first boyfriend in third grade, my first kiss in sixth grade, and was well into the world of dating and make-out sessions by eighth grade. I struggled to understand and accept my sexuality. It, too, was shrouded in shame and silence. As with anatomy and femininity, I was self-conscious and confused about the mystery of sex. I knew it was something my body felt a natural inclination toward, and yet I felt deep shame and fear that such urges existed within me.

In those early teen years, I dipped my toe into the waters of sexual expression, but always felt a sense of restriction and shame when I did. Like my period, sexuality felt like the unwelcome guest, a force to be restrained and subdued at all costs. And so, in my later teen years, I switched to a strict abstinence, only seeing sexuality and sexual expression in a negative light. I repented repeatedly for the kisses I'd bestowed in my earlier days and carried a sense of brokenness for being a sexual being at all. I hated the sexual attention I received for my curves, so much so that at age twenty one, I had breast-reduction surgery in an attempt to minimize my femininity and sexuality. I did not want the curves, the desires or the attention.

By the time I reached college, the regularity of menstruation had broken down much of the stigma and shame surrounding it. I learned to purchase a box of tampons without spiraling into a total panic. I entered friendships with more liberated women who ushered me into a world of open chatter about our bodies and our sexuality. I engaged in these conversations, still with flushed cheeks and a sense of scandal, but also with a growing acceptance of my female self. An acceptance I am still working out today.

~:~

Perhaps it was the restriction of those earlier days and the shame of the unspoken that has lead me as a mother to speak so openly with my own children today. Or perhaps it is the fact that, in becoming a mother, my body careened into a world of indiscretion: the act of sex announced openly and embraced with celebration, legs spread wide for repeated inspection, a rounding belly announcing my femininity and sexuality to the world. Each time I felt my baby kick inside, I sensed a deeper beauty and magic to my sexuality than I had ever dared imagine before. Each time my body and its functions were spoken of directly, respectfully, naturally, I felt wholeness and freedom increase. Each time a new mother nursed her baby from full, unashamed breast, I felt strength and courage rise within me.

When my daughter, Havyn, was born just eleven months after my son, Kyler, we soon found ourselves in a world of openly declaring the anatomy and functions of the female and male bodies. The kids, now two and three, have always bathed together and thus became quickly aware of the anatomical differences between each other. When asked, we have spoken with frankness and respect. A penis has always and only been called a *penis* in our home. A vagina has always and only been called a *vagina* in our home. These terms are used daily and freely, with no mystery or shame attached.

The result, thus far, is not only a stigma-free acceptance of their bodies and their differences, but a plethora of funny stories. For example, in the bath the other night, the kids were swimming and splashing around as usual. My son found himself on his back, wiggling back and forth, enjoying the waves he was creating. I looked away to my husband briefly, who soon directed my attention with a pointed finger back toward my son. When I met my son's eyes, he declared, *"Look mama! The penis is dancing!"* Sure enough, his wiggles were carrying through his entire body, giving every part of his little anatomy their own life and movement.

Earlier that week, on our way to a friend's house for a playdate, my daughter announced that she was feeding her baby doll. When I looked in the rearview mirror, I discovered her with lifted shirt, baby facing her belly. *"Oh, I see. Was your baby hungry?"* I asked. *"Yep! See, she's eating from my belly button!"* two-year-old Havyn proudly declared. We had just done a homeschooling unit on babies - baby animals and all the different ways they are born and fed and nurtured. It quickly became obvious that the lesson on a baby feeding from their own belly button in utero had gotten jumbled together in her little brain with the lesson on a baby feeding from their mother's breast once outside the womb. I tried to re-explain the different feeding scenarios in two-year-old terms. In doing so, my son realized a hole in my explanation: First the baby is *in* the womb, then she's *out*.

"Um, mama, so how does the baby get out?!" he asked. I avoided the question at first, partially reverting to my earlier days of discretion and silence, and partially trying to decide what I thought was an appropriate response. When he asked a second time, however, my voice and courage returned and I simply said, *"Well, the baby comes out if its mama's vagina."* I was able to capture his initial expression in the rearview mirror, which was a priceless mixture of surprise and terror. *"Does that seem weird to you, buddy?"* I asked calmly in response to his face. His surprised expression remained as he nodded his head up and down in affirmation. *"I know, I thought it was really weird, too! It's pretty amazing that a woman's body can do that, huh?"* I replied. His face softened, at which time I got to glance at my daughter for the first time since the announcement. She was busy repositioning her baby at her breast to eat.

A few minutes later we arrived for our playdate. When my dear friend opened the door to greet us, Kyler proudly announced, *"Ms. Whitney, did you know that babies come out of their mama's vaginas?!"* His expression had transitioned now to one of amusement and awe, like he was carrying with him news of the world's greatest miracle. *Which, in many senses, he was.* Whitney was one of those beautifully liberated women I met back in my college days, and so she received the announcement with great calmness and esteem. *"You're right, Kyler! What do you think of that?!"* she asked enthusiastically. He paused briefly, then simply said, *"Good!"* The rest of the playdate went on without any further mentioning of babies or vaginas.

Later that night, Kyler made his grand announcement to his daddy. Once again his words were received with openness and wonder. And still today, he speaks with calmness and confidence about the birthing process. And here's what I see: We - parents, teachers, adults, society - shape a child's outlook on *everything.* As amazing and intelligent and perceptive as my son may be, the reality is unavoidable that all the positive responses he received from the adults he most respects that day shaped his own outlook on the subject. Had I avoided his curiosity entirely, he could have begun to attach a negative stigma of shame around his question, or even questioning in general. Had we responded with make believe words or fairy tale-ish explanations of the birthing process, we would have been setting him on the same path of future confusion, fear and embarrassment around the subject that I myself had walked down for so long. Had our responses carried correction, shock or awkward looks, he, too, would have learned to tip-toe around the subject.

~:~

Only time will tell for sure, but I have to believe that by framing our responses to Kyler that day in openness and positive enthusiasm, he was lovingly introduced to one of life's most natural, most miraculous acts, and will continue to treat it without shame or fear.

I know that not all will agree with me on this frankness method. Our outlooks and parenting decisions are so intricately impacted by our own childhoods and experiences throughout life, that it would be nearly impossible for any two people to completely agree on such a sensitive subject. I think beauty often lies in the balancing act of avoiding either extreme: overly-sharing versus silence, make-believe terminology verses age inappropriate dialogue. My goal is not to raise children ahead of their ages, fully aware of every bodily or sexual function. My goal is also not to answer every single question my children ask with complete disclosure. I think there will be times when an answer like, *"Well, I can tell you XYZ, but the rest will have to wait until you are older. Let's talk about it again in a few years."* will be the best possible response I can give them, that I *do*, now, give to them. Offering them reality in language and doses that their maturity and age can handle, to me, is an invaluable gift of love.

It seems, if nothing else, life has shown me the value of speaking - *nothing off limits* - of letting your voice be heard, of calling things as they are, with humility and love and respect. **That silence suffocates, allowing shame to grow and fear to fester.** But talking, communing openly and deeply with those we know and love the most - whether about our bodies, the birthing process or some burning question about life - is a truly holy act. And so, in our family, we choose to speak.

Writing Prompt: Write about the way your body, your gender and your sexuality were spoken of as a child, and how that has affected your views today. Consider: What topics in your family were *"off limits"*? What would it mean to begin putting words to those hidden or shamed areas?

THE FUNDAMENTALS

*It is as if what we're going through is almost too real and too raw
to bring up at church. But if you can't bring up matters of life and
death and God's Spirit here, where can you? Maybe it's because
we are accustomed to dealing with issues in tidy chunks. We
grapple, but we do it during a twenty-minute sermon, a
twelve-week class, a topic scheduled six to eight months
in advance. There is nothing tidy about a child dying.*

Anna Whiston-Donaldson, *Rare Bird*

I was raised, like many middle-class Caucasian Americans,
as an evangelical Christian. Every Sunday morning, my
mother would coax the five of us into our *"Sunday best"* and
drive us twenty minutes to Sunday School, where we
learned about Jonah and the whale, Jesus feeding the five
thousand and Noah's great ark, through crafts and songs
and snacks. Our Sunday School was held in a daycare
building that the church rented for the weekend. After
learning that Jesus died to cleanse me of all my sin as long
as I asked him into my heart *(which I did repeatedly)*, and that
Paul showed us a good Christian is willing to speak boldly
and confidently about the Gospel *(which I never quite mastered)*,
my attention was increasingly diverted to the shelves of toys
and the large outdoor playground that seemed to wave at
me through all the windows surrounding the room. My
most vivid Sunday School memories are of hiding in the
tunnel slide while others looked all over for me, running

with mulch in my shoes, climbing and chasing until our *"Sunday best"* were full of dust and our cheeks were the shade of an evening sunset.

At home, my mother did her best at Biblical parenting: praying with us before bedtime, protecting us from evil influences, making sure we attended VBS every year. I remember with fondness my mother lying on the floor beside our bunk beds, listening to us rattle on about our days. As a mother myself now, I realize how exhausted she must have been come bedtime, how desperate for a moment alone, a moment's rest. But I have strong memories of her staying with us until we fell asleep, sharing stories and then praying together, *"As I lay me down to sleep, I pray the Lord my soul to keep. I know God watches over me and keeps me safe from night to day. Thank you, Jesus, for loving me. Amen."* That bedtime routine remained a comforting security throughout my childhood.

I remember, too, many Halloween nights cramming with my sisters beside our bedroom window in our dark house, watching all the neighborhood children walk from door-to-door, giggling in their festive costumes. My mother was adamantly against the celebration of Halloween, known in our home as "The Devil's Birthday." She would keep us home from school whichever day all the Halloween celebrations were to happen, and on trick-or-treat night she would turn off all the house lights and shut the curtains at dusk. The sight of little princesses and ninjas collecting buckets of candy looked like *fun* to me, but my mother insisted it was evil.

One year around Halloween, I remember my mother taking us to the mall to play on an indoor playground - and probably to appease some built-up frustration that we kids were lashing out at her for her refusal to allow us to dress up or collect candy. The mall seemed particularly busy, and we should have guessed something was up after watching the fourth Dorothy walk into the mall as we circled again for a parking space, but so desperate were we all for an evening of fun that we tromped in anyway. *Right into the Devil's Birthday Party itself.*

Much to our dismay, we found out it was trick-or-treat night at the mall, and we were perhaps the only children in attendance without costumes or buckets to collect treats. As I remember, we still got to play, but the big indoor slide wasn't nearly as sweet to zip down when you were the only child without a lollipop in your mouth while doing it.

Much of my mother's desire to protect us from evil was directed toward the movies and shows we watched. Popular shows of the 80's like *The Smurfs* and *Care Bears* were off-limits because they promoted sorcery. Once, we went on a rare outing to the movies to watch *Fern Gully,* and were quickly escorted back out of our seats twenty minutes in when "Mother Nature" - characterized as a magical tree - started talking. I remember with shock and horror being rushed out of that dark theater, something about the evil of magic being whispered into my ear. Later, my mother turned on one of our favorites, *The Kingdom Chums*, a movie where three children are magically transported to a land of talking animals whose mission is to help children memorize the Ten Commandments with sweet melodies. As a child, I never understood why talking trees were from the devil, but talking animals were from God.

~:~

At the ripe old age of twelve, I began to fret constantly about the eternal state of my soul. Having heard almost weekly for the former decade of my life about heaven and hell, those "in" and those "out," I was growing increasingly uncomfortable about not knowing for sure that I was "in." One night, attending an evening revival service with my best friend and her family, I listened attentively to the yellow-haired, charismatic preacher. I listened to words I had heard many times before, but for the first time, it seemed my cognitive maturity had finally caught up and the words started to *make sense.* I was a sinner, born depraved and with an evil nature. I would live and die in this state: sinful, flawed, stained in the sight of the perfect God who made me, forever banished from His presence - *unless* I confessed that all these things about me were true and that Jesus was my only escape. *Unless* I prayed, with sincerity, that Jesus come live in my heart, cleanse me of my sinful nature, and help me live a life pleasing to God. *Then* I would be allowed in heaven and God would welcome me as his child. *Then* God's grand love would fill my heart and make me good. *Then* I could call Him Father.

I walked down the aisle when the yellow-haired preacher asked if anyone wasn't sure where they would go when they died; when the yellow-haired preacher asked if anyone needed someone to save them from their sins and present them as perfect before God; when the yellow-haired preacher asked if anyone wanted to invite Jesus into their hearts and start a life in the Love of God. I walked down the aisle of that old Methodist church, creaky wooden floors and crimson pews in neat rows, tears streaming down my face, cheeks burning with tween emotions. I walked down the aisle, desperate to guarantee, once and for all, that I was *"in."* Desperate to be made good. Desperate for a loving Father.

Immediately, I started attending youth group every week and followed a reading plan to get through the Bible in a year. I was passionate, excited, committed - what we called "on fire for God." I spent the next several years doing everything in my power to "fan the flame" - attending weekend conferences, leading Bible studies, showing up at church every time the doors were open. My skirts got longer and my shirts looser, I threw out all my old CDs and replaced them with Barlow Girls and Jars of Clay. I kissed dating goodbye, went on missions trips and attended See You at the Pole. I did prayer walks around my high school, tried to memorize all the right answers and share them with my friends, organized church potlucks and parades. I sat in the front row and took notes throughout the sermon each Sunday.

After my senior year of high school, I moved to Texas for a yearlong Christian leadership experience. During my first week, I was handed an enormous, dark green book called, *How Now Shall We Live*, a book explaining all the ins-and-outs of a Christian worldview, which I studied diligently and thoroughly. I learned why Buddhism was flawed, why evolution was wrong, why only those who believed in "Biblical Christianity" were right and therefore going to heaven. I soon was convinced that there was in fact an answer to *every* question, and that I was on the winning team that knew them all.

Rachel Held Evans describes my decade as a Christian perfectly when she writes in her book, *Faith Unraveled: "I used to be a fundamentalist. Not the Teletubby-hating, apocalypse-ready, Jerry Falwell type of fundamentalist, but the kind who thinks that God is pretty much figured out already, that he's done telling us anything new. I was fundamentalist in the sense that I thought salvation means having the right opinions about God and that fighting the good fight of faith requires defending those opinions at all costs. I was a fundamentalist because my security and self-worth and sense of purpose in life were all wrapped up in getting God right - in believing the right things about him, saying the right things about him, and convincing others to embrace the right things about him, too."*

~:~

The truth is, no matter how many answers I memorized, no matter how many hours I prayed, no matter how many new Bible verses I stored up in my heart, I always had doubts. I remember very early on in my faith - within a year of my encounter with that yellow-haired preacher - feeling so unsure about the reality of God and how little I seemed to sense Him, that I often cried myself to sleep to Nichole Nordeman's, *To Know You.* She sings about the proof that Thomas needed, and the questions that keep her awake at night. It was the only safe place I found for expressing my struggle with doubts and all the questions that stirred in me. And so I turned Nichole up really loud, sobbing and singing my struggles with her.

A couple years later, I would experience my first real faith crisis during my senior year of high school when hours and hours of pre-dawn prayer walking seemed to bear no fruit. Reeling from this disappointment, I spiraled further into disillusionment when a mission trip I had been planning to go on, just weeks later, got canceled and re-routed to a totally different country. With little time for planning, the trip turned out to be a logistical nightmare. With no translators, we spent the entire month - you guessed it - *prayer walking.* Occasionally we would find someone who spoke English and would plow through the Romans Road (a tool used in conversion) with them, only to find our listener calmly uninterested. Even when I exaggerated everything I felt and believed to make the Gospel seem *"too good to pass up,"* the listener remained completely unmoved, adding to my own doubts and questions and insecurities.

I came home from that mission trip - where 100 teenagers spent a month overseas and did not earn a single "salvation badge" - wondering if my prayers made any difference, wondering why I didn't feel more confident about the Good News I was supposed to be sharing, wondering if God even existed. I remember voicing my struggle very generally with a friend, and although she was understanding and kind in her response, I got the sense that these were questions that the church at large was not willing or able to deal with. I am not sure if it was ever explicitly said, but the unanimous feeling in our Christian community was that doubting was bad and that believing the right things with full confidence was essential to being a good Christian. And so, I felt ashamed of my doubts, frustrated with my unbelief, desperate to be "on fire" again.

I would cycle through these faith crises every couple of years, somehow finding a way to stuff all the questions back into a corner and move ahead with all my religious activity again, often with a renewed sense of purpose and devotion as a Christian. These were always very private struggles, very shame-laden seasons, where I would remove myself from ministry and the church for a short season until I could muster up enough faith to be sure and believe all the right things again. In every doubt, in every uncertainty and question, I felt less-than and never heard voices of peers or leadership give me a reason to think otherwise.

~:~

Then came the biggest faith crisis of all. Earth-shattering, life-altering, foundation-crumbling. After losing our first son, I could not stop the avalanche of questions that broke open in my heart. I couldn't stuff all that doubt and pain and disillusionment back into a corner, a corner that was already full from all those earlier years of stifling so many questions and insecurities. I could not stop wondering, *"Why?"* and wrestling with theological issues like heaven and hell, God's sovereignty and our free will, prayer and the character of God.

And so I didn't. I didn't stop asking, I didn't stuff the questions away. I voiced them, for the first time ever, and it freaked everyone out, including myself. Nobody knew what to do with an "on fire" Christian, fresh off the mission field, wrestling with the existence of God. At first, friends and leaders seemed comfortable enough to attribute all the asking and wrestling to our grief, and equally comfortable assuming that this was a season that we would pass through soon enough. Few people engaged with the actual questions or doubts themselves, but instead prayed that we would have enough faith to make it through the mountain of grief we were experiencing.

Unfortunately, we weren't able to make it through that mountain of grief fast enough, and so soon empathetic eyes turned into judgmental glances. I was told multiple times that because I was questioning God and the Bible so deeply, I was obviously not a Christian to begin with. So intense was our church community's need for answers and obsession with right belief, that very few were able to allow us space for questioning. None seemed even aware that whole segments of the Body of Christ honor Mystery as a name for the Divine, or that whole communities were devoted to the idea of voicing every question in the pursuit of fuller Truth and in embracing uncertainty as a necessary virtue.

I wouldn't hear the names Barbara Taylor Brown or Rachel Held Evans until years later. I wouldn't learn that being a Christian has historically and internationally worked itself out with incredible diversity, much of which has little resemblance to many evangelical churches today. I would not know that the Body of Christ is like a rare multi-faceted diamond, looking a bit different from each angle, yet still one. I would not realize, for a few lonely years, that being a Christian and having doubts are in no way mutually exclusive. That there were "on fire" Christians saying things like, *"When we require that all people must say the same words or subscribe to the same creeds in order to experience God, we underestimate the scope and power of God's activity in the world.*

Gone are the black-and-white categories of "saved" and "unsaved," "heaven-bound" and "hell-bound." Gone are the security of absolutism and the comfort of certainty....But the assurance that I can still be a Christian without believing that God hates the world and damns most of it to hell gave me just enough hope to jump onto the next lily pad on my way across the swamp of doubt."[3]

Mercifully, I learned that God *is* bigger than my narrow "Christian" worldview had ever allowed. I learned that the church has never looked one "right" way, and that Jesus himself spoke most sharply against fellow Jewish leaders who were too caught up in all the answers and all the black and whites to see the humanity of those around them. I learned that certainty is an illusion, that an answer to every question was never the point, *that Mystery and faith are what I have been after all along.*

Writing Prompt: What certainties have you become less sure of over the years? How have your fundamentals - about life, relationships, about the Divine - altered or changed completely? Where could you use more flexibility in your pursuit of God?

---

3 *Faith Unraveled,* Rachel Held Evans

INDIA

We're all made up of the same amount of God.
Glennon Doyle Melton, *Carry On Warrior*

When I was sixteen, I attended a Christian conference with my youth group for the weekend, called "Aquire the Fire." We traveled in a large, white church van, listened to Christian pop music and chattered with excitement in our matching tie-dyed t-shirts. We were a buoyant cloud of peachy pink, jubilantly making our way to an enormous venue where we gathered with thousands of other matching t-shirt teen groups.

It was the first time I experienced the Christianity of professional lighting and stage effects, deafening volumes and mass crowds. It was also the first time I experienced the emotional enrapturing of modern evangelical worship music - bass drum beating, beautiful voices belting, hands raised, lights lowered. I was totally taken with the enormity, the camaraderie, the wonder and power of standing beside thousands of my peers in this sort of worship.

At the conference, we were shown a video about people in need from around the world. The appeal was for their souls, for our reaching them with the *"Message of the Cross"* before it was too late. I couldn't help but notice their physical need as well - the discrepancy in their clothing, their housing, their boney-faced, missing-tooth smiles from what all us middle class, mostly white teens in the auditorium experienced as our daily reality. We knew comfy beds and designer jeans and all-you-can-eat buffets. Our existence was worlds apart from theirs.

The deeper reality, however, the more important crisis, we were told, was their eternal destinies. The ensnaring religions these people followed, religions and practices that it seemed had helped lead these countries to their dire states, needed replaced with our westernized Christian faith. The message was clear: fix their spiritual state and everything else would fall into place. It's what today I see as a tragically skewed, "*We're right and they're wrong*" Gospel, a modern-day appeal to colonize the savage lands. But at the time, all I could see was one dark, starving stare after another, peering at me from those enormous screens, whispering, *Help*.

Beyond genuine compassion and beyond the skewed religion tugging at my heart as I watched face after native-face flash in front of me, I sensed a further pull, another force drawing me to action. Perhaps louder than the message that these souls needed saved, was the message that *I* was the one called to do it. That God had commanded me, *needed me*, to go to the ends of the earth for this very job; that the committed, the brave, the willing servant would leave everything and go preach the "*Good News.*" Naturally, then, my performance-prone, people-pleasing teen heart stood erect when an invitation was made to travel to one of these destitute countries, ministering to lost souls and fulfilling the Great Commission. It seemed like an obvious next step in my recent conversion to Christianity, an obvious step toward pleasing my heavenly Father. And so when the words, *"Stand if you are willing for God to use you..."* were spoken, I jumped to my feet.

Moments after, I looked through the missions brochure, reading descriptions of every country the organization lead teen trips to, heart a-swirl with hopes of achievement, of affecting change, of satisfying the Divine. Each country had a "ministry difficulty" rating as well as a "physical difficulty" rating, with ten points total denoting the most resistant culture and strenuous of circumstances. I flipped through, page after page, searching for the highest combined rating I could find. I filled out the interest slip with passion and commitment, and checked the box for India, whose profile was rated a perfect ten.

When the conference was over, we all loaded up and headed back to our small, conservative church in our small, conservative town. No stage effects, no drums or guitars, no big screens or lowered lights. It was a beautifully simple church that honored us youth and often gave us a platform to speak during the service. And so the Sunday following our weekend away, several of us lined up in front of the hundred or so people that made up our congregation, and shared about our impassioning conference experiences.

After watching that video with all the dark stares, many in our youth group had stood up in commitment to go, and so now we each, in turn, spoke of our desire to travel overseas that following summer. I remember listening to my peers, standing in a row, speaking one by one, *"I'd like to go to South America this summer,"* *"If God provides, I'm hoping to travel to Africa,"* - and then my turn came. I remember vividly the determination that filled my heart, the physical certainty that took over my body as I said, *"I am going to India for two months this summer."* My emphasis spoke louder than the words and in my heart, it was as good as done.

I do not remember ever asking my parents for permission to go to India. I was mentally so many steps toward those whispers for *Help* by the time we got home, however, it would have been hard for anyone to have stopped me. The thousands of dollars that needed raised did not phase me, the thousands of miles and endless plane hours that needed traversed only excited me more. I was a ball of total commitment and absolute certainty, riding the high of true devotion and compassion, mixed with a lifelong addiction to achievement.

All that winter and spring, I fundraised and prayed and dreamed. I studied the culture and the language and bought lots of long skirts and travel-sized toiletries. My friends and family were extremely supportive and through the hard work of our youth group and the generosity of many, all the necessary money came in, all the needed shots were administered, all the required plane tickets were purchased.

~:~

At seventeen, just a few days after finishing my Junior year of high school, I boarded a plane for the first time in my life and headed, alone, to Texas. I spent a week in Texas, meeting my leaders and teammates and learning a skit that would be the main ministry tool we utilized once in India. There were more powerful, emotionally-charged worship sessions and more stirring calls to commitment and soul-saving. Again, I felt overcome with the camaraderie of something so much bigger than myself, with the privilege of being *needed* for something so important.

We were nearly one hundred teens, with a few adult leaders, excitedly traveling to a third world country. The flights were long and the layovers chaotic. Although I had studied a bit about the culture and learned more with my team in Texas, nothing could have prepared me for all the sights and sounds and smells I would encounter once disembarking the plane in Bangalore.

The airport was humid and stale. It was quiet and relatively empty. Men in uniform were stoically positioned in every corner, whispering and snickering in a language I could not begin to understand. As we headed toward the exit - a mass of light-skinned, tired teens - the rush to my senses was indescribable. Overwhelming smells of spice and sweat, vibrant colors of gorgeously draped saris and large billboards, deafening volumes of beeping horns, rushing cars and masses of men, women and children reaching for us from every direction. I was astonished by the quantity of people, the crowding of bodies so tight that our leaders had to push a single-file path for us in order to get to our bus. Brushing and bumping against those dark stares I had seen so many months ago, I felt I had been transported in time, to another world, to another life.

Once on the bus, I was silent with wonder, my senses working double-time to try to take in all that was new. Everywhere I turned there was something startling to see. Women digging in piles of dung, their day's work to make fuel patties; elderly men, with every bone in their body showing through sun-darkened skin, pulling large loads on wonky rickshaws; young children, with even younger children strapped to their backs, begging for food; ornate Hindu temples with their array of foreign gods proudly standing at every corner. It was rich and devastating and alive and dead all at once. It was impossible to take it all in.

Finally, my eyes rested on a group of women, with piercing brown eyes, bright floral saris and waste-length black braids. Every one of them seemed to be adorned with at least a few gold bangles, some with dozens. They wore bindis on their foreheads and jewels in their noses. I - a self-conscious, body-loathing American teen - sat breathless, nearly suffocated by their beauty.

The bus zoomed and swerved and honked down a half-finished highway, leading us to the Catholic retreat center that would be our home for the next two months. The center, Claret Nivas, was quiet and serene, surrounded by thick trees and well-manicured gardens. There were endless trails and benches and places to hide and think for hours. I recall it today with longing, remembering the peace and beauty and people of that place.

We unloaded and were assigned to our rooms. Each room was a small square concrete enclosure, with two cots and a tiny sink in the corner. We were four to a room, rotating turns on the floor in sleeping bags. In a separate building, there was a large meeting space, where we had daily worship and teachings, and also a dining hall, where I got my first taste of Indian curry and authentic chai tea.

There was construction going on at the retreat center the entire two months that we were living there. Some addition to the large meeting space, being erected by migrant workers whose families were housed in tiny, make-shift huts beside the construction site. I was too young and naive, too inexperienced and caught up in the zeal of our soul-saving mission to quite take in the reality that stood before me. But when I think about it today, I realize these were multi-generational families of six, seven, eight people, housed in tin shacks no more than ten feet long by six feet deep. One room black holes, smaller than most bedrooms, housing at least half a dozen people.

I never got to enter those specific shacks, but was invited into many other homes throughout villages in India. I was constantly amazed by the generosity and hospitality with which we were welcomed. Once, a dozen or more of us were invited by an older woman into a tiny hut, made of mud and tin. I do not remember there being any furniture in her home, just a plastic mat covering the main sitting area. Yet despite her obvious poverty, this woman was so eager to love us and feed us that she cut up all the fruit she had on hand – which happened to be three rotten mangoes. I remember sitting there, struggling to swallow my bite of squishy, sour mango, watching her vibrant eyes and generous smile, seeing how thankful she was to have anything at all to offer us.

In other villages, young women eagerly offered me their bangles, adorning my arms and giggling at how much larger my hands were than theirs. We constantly found trays of chai being passed around for us to consume or bunches of bananas being given for our journey home. *Over and over and over again, we were met with generosity, acceptance and love.*

Perhaps the greatest example of this was in the children of the migrant workers at our retreat center. Despite all the people and all the culture we experienced during our two months throughout India, I was most affected by those children. There were three girls that I was particularly drawn to, and them to me. One was around the age of 8, one closer to 12 and another only three-years-old. I am not sure how you would properly spell their names, but phonetically they sound like Jayanti, Sarala and Divya. Those names have stuck permanently in my mind for the past fifteen years, lodged in my heart and frequently surfacing to remind me of the connection we shared. I can see their faces in my mind's eye – kindness in their smiles, courage in their hands, acceptance in their eyes.

When the older two were not busy with chores or assisting their families at the construction site, they would all wander toward our dorms, waiting shyly by a tree or playing discreetly in the dirt, just within view. I can see their tattered, faded clothes, their dark skin and curious eyes, their black braids and bright smiles. I can hear their giggles, see their timid glances before they knew they were allowed to show themselves freely. In my memory, Claret Nivas is consumed with the presence of those three beauties, with no first interaction and no moment when we weren't deeply connected.

I was soon so in love with these girls, and them with me, that many mornings we would sit on a bench in one of the gardens for an hour, or more, looking at each other, giggling, playing with each other's hair, learning words from one another, smiling and holding hands. Theirs were the first faces I looked for in the mornings and the first I ran to when we returned in the evenings. We became so comfortable with one another, that the girls would often sit on my lap or lay on my shoulder in silence while I read a book or wrote in my journal. We experienced a connection that transcended language, transcended culture or religion or any "should" we previously knew.

~:~

It would be another decade before I would experience my own faith crisis, as Rachel Held Evans describes so wittily in her book, *Searching For Sunday*, *"I was raised evangelical, which means I spent a good part of my life feeling sorry for the rest of humanity on account of its certain destiny in hell. This was not something my parents taught me directly, just something I picked up from preachers, Sunday school teachers, and Christian playmates along the way. After hearing time and again that "wide is the path that leads to destruction," I just assumed that Buddhists went to hell for worshipping Buddha, Catholics went to hell for worshipping Mary, and Al Gore went to hell for worshipping nature. I didn't even think to have a faith crisis about it until college."*

After India, I spent the next decade of my life living with these harsh religious beliefs of, *"You're in or you're out,"* running around trying to earn and prove and obey every rule, following a form of faith that skewed love for law. And yet, those three little Indian girls planted a seed of acceptance and truth in my heart that would eventually take root. Their kindness and generosity, all these years later, sings to me of the beauty of humanity, of the divine seed in each of us. Their love reminds me of what the late Maya Angelou was often quoted as saying, *"No experience ever goes wasted."* That despite all that was lacking in my heart at the time, all that was wrong in my motives and skewed in my perspective, India – Jayanthi, Sarala and Divya - were a part of my becoming, another thread of grace beautifully woven into the story of my life, making me who I am today.

Writing Prompt: Write about a time you experienced people very different from yourself - *a different economic class, different culture, different religion or different social class.* In what ways, now, can you see similarities? What did those differences teach you?

LISTS

Transcendence makes our tragedies look smaller and opens us to the possibility that life is more than tragedy and that there is also grace, which is given in the miracle of the present moment.

Jerry Sittser, *A Grace Disguised*

Last fall I felt a sudden itch to write a bucket list. Like many who have experienced the shock of a tragic death, I was filled with a sense of urgency to live life more fully and an uncertainty as to how many more days I would have left to do that. Having always been prone to making lists, a bucket list seemed like a logical next step in trying to seize each day and fully embrace every moment. Plus, I was aching for some sense of control in these numbered days, some charted route toward fulfillment and meaning despite all of life's hardships and losses.

I kept my husband up late one evening with grandiose plans of creating truly epic bucket lists that would satisfy all our yearnings for a full life, a connected life, a meaningful life (I say this only slightly tongue-in-cheek). With such high expectations, it may be no surprise that I ended the night disappointed and still directionless. Within fifteen minutes of starting our brainstorming session, it became obvious that there was very little that excited me, very few things that I could look to as dreams I had always wanted to see fulfilled or cared about investing any energy at all into. My ever-supportive husband tried to encourage me and rally me back to the cause, but I quickly lost heart. I thought and thought and then with a heavy sigh threw down the fruit of a half-hour of labor:

1) Complete a triathlon
2) Run a half marathon
3) ~~Travel to~~
4)
5)

The next day I woke up thinking about our bucket-list-failure and trying to figure out why it had been so hard to come up with ideas and goals. I mused, *Am I clinically depressed, is that why I can't think of more than two things in life that truly, deeply excite me?* I was currently in counseling for a myriad of reasons, least of which was the recent death of my brother's girlfriend and the less-recent loss of our foster son. I knew there was some truth to the fact that life's tragedies were over-shadowing life's joys. *But that is exactly why I had wanted to make the list.* That is exactly why I had felt so compelled to take back some control of my life and at least set its aim toward things that mattered to me. I was not willing to let depression or loss or death have the last word.

Later, I wondered if the weight of calling something a *life goal* was impairing in and of itself. Maybe attaching so much importance to coming up with each item on the list was my problem. Maybe that lurking perfectionist in me shied away from such an epic task. Maybe I needed to simplify, to step back and look at the list with different eyes.

The next evening, on a walk with my youngest sister, I was given those new eyes. She told me about a *"101 Things to Do in 1001 Days"* list she had made a few months earlier. The list was intended to be a cross between a bucket list and a to-do list...meaningful, magical, but also practical and plausible. Since every item should be checked off within three and a half years, the list should not carry the weight of a bucket list. Some goals would be bigger than others, some take more time, more money, more focus than others. But some would be simple, silly, even mundane.

I latched onto the *"101 Things in 1001 Days"* list and started brainstorming mine later that evening. It took a few days to come up with all 101, but I noticed that the more I wrote, the more things I was excited about doing. The easier it was to find things I really cared about. Once I reached number 101, I had to choose between several remaining possibilities. What had seemed like a dark abyss inside me just a week earlier was now an overflowing fountain of goals and ideas and things to be excited about living toward.

My list ranged from as simple as *"Learn the postal workers' names"* to as adventurous and vague as *"Travel West."* It was as silly as *"Dance in the rain,"* as intentional as *"Read 30 new books"* and as meaningful as *"Say I love you when it's hard."* I thought about the people I loved the most, the values I held closest, the causes that impassioned me deeply. I thought about when I felt the most alive and the truest to myself. I thought about how I could love best and give back the most. *I thought about looking back on life, at the end, and wrote toward all the things I'd like to see there.* One by one, I wrote 101 things that I knew would make my life fuller, richer, better.

~:~

It has been a year since I jotted 101 items on a piece of notebook paper, then had my husband type and print them, and finally gave the list its permanent home on our refrigerator. I see the list multiple times a day, sometimes in hurried obscurity, but often with intention and anticipation. I check in with the list, make plans based on the list. Today, it has dates marked in blue and black and red ink all over it. Time stamps of meaningful memories.

"Design an art room," seated as number two on my list, is checked off with an exclamation point and a large 10/1/13, marking the day we moved our master bedroom into the small front office and turned the original master bedroom into a wonderful space for art and learning. We built a custom four by eight foot table with lots of side storage, stocked full of paper and paint and glue and crayons. We hung art, made art, and now spend hours in that room every day, creating and learning as a family.

"Watch 'Selena' and 'Wild Hearts Can't Be Broken'" is checked off with 12/28/13 and 1/9/14, the days I got to watch these old childhood favorites thanks to DVD Christmas gifts from my husband. *"Play mini golf"* and *"Take Kyler on a date"* are both marked with 10/6/13, for the afternoon Kyler and I got dressed up and headed to the range together. *"Ride a train"* is time stamped 10/23/13, the day the kids and I boarded our zoo's little train and experienced the wonder of wildlife by rail.

"Make Thai food" is checked and dated 5/30/14, for the night our Cooking Club went with a Thai theme and I made Tom Kha soup for the first time in years. Another friend made the most delicious peanut curry and the host's brother made fresh spring rolls with an incredible sesame dipping sauce. There was Thai iced tea and fresh mango slices and chocolate for dessert. We nearly licked every plate and pan clean.

"Restore a piece of furniture" is marked 10/2/13, for those two old school desks that were hand-me-downed to me and now have fresh coats of white paint on the legs and black chalk paint on the tops. *"Buy fresh flowers for the house for a month in winter"* was checked off last March, when I kept a simple bouquet of the beautiful outdoors on our kitchen table all month. *"Surprise a friend with a 'Just Because'"* is dated 11/11/13, for the day the kids and I bought a cartful of cleaning supplies and household items, then delivered them to dear friends who had recently moved into their new home.

"Expand the garden" is time stamped in black, 5/1/14, the day we all tilled the ground and planted rows of snap peas and cucumbers seeds and dug holes for the tomato and pepper plants. The kids and I watched in awe in the weeks that followed as, slowly but surely, little green sprouts appeared through the clay and despite our gardening deficiencies, we gathered baskets full of fresh vegetables. Many batches of fresh salsa and fiesta bean salad were consumed that summer thanks to our harvest.

"Bake Christmas cookies as a family" is time stamped 12/6/13, for the day my husband's family had their traditional cookie

baking day, where we each bring ingredients for our favorite cookie and then bake dozens and dozens of Christmas treats to share with one another. The house is full of busy toddlers with sticky hands running all around, some adults relaxing with a cup of coffee in the living room while their goodies bake and others covered in flour and piles of measuring cups and ingredients at the kitchen table. The house is warm and noisy and full of people I love. At the end of the day, every flat surface is piled high with rows of sugar cookies and macaroons, towers of buckeyes and coconut balls, tins full of chocolate-covered pretzels and salted caramels. After taking our traditional group shot behind the obscenity of sweets, we each fill multiple Tupperware to the brim with goodies to be shared with friends and coworkers in the week to come.

Beside *"Make one sustainable lifestyle change"* is written 7/8/14, for the day I purchased our little compost pail by the sink and my husband assembled our large compost barrel out back. *"Go paddle boating"* is dated in green, 7/10/14, the hot summer day we braved the waters of Alum Creek and took the kids on their first paddle boat ride. *"Reconnect with an old friend"* is lovingly dated 11/5/13, the first day I had coffee with my old high school friends, Julie and Sarah, who had recently moved back to Columbus. Now, we share playdates with Julie and her kids weekly, spend special events together and have become regular parts of each other's lives.

To date, 350 days after making the *"101 Things"* list, I have checked off just over half the items. The list has become part of our family, a catalyst toward so many beautiful shared memories. I feel a surprising sense of direction and fulfillment from the list - not because the list is magical in and of itself, but *because it has oriented me toward all the things that are already most valuable and meaningful to me.* Where before the busyness of life would have normally whisked me away into the mundane and less meaningful, this little list has helped me stay focused on my priorities, on the people and causes I love the most.

Number 98 on my list reads *"Inspire someone else to make a list."* Maybe today you can help me add a time stamp to that one?

Writing Prompt: Compile your own *"101 Things in 1001 Days"* list. Think of the people you love, the things that make you smile, the sights and smells that make you breath deeper. In three years, what would bring you great joy to be able to look back and see?

UNLESS

To let ourselves sink into the joyful moments of our lives even though we know that they are fleeting, even though the world tells us not to be too happy lest we invite disaster - that's an intense form of vulnerability.

Brené Brown, *Daring Greatly*

I do not feel over-the-top in the slightest when I say that I have the most amazing husband I have ever met. It feels more like fact than opinion, nothing that could be seen as arrogance, nothing that has *anything* to do with me. *Simple, objective truth.*

My husband serves and he gives and he loves and he affirms. He cleans and he cooks, he cares and he considers. He frequently tells me how thankful he is that I stay home with our kids, how amazing that half-charred dinner was, how lovely my three-days-without-a-shower face is. He requires me to rest and to enjoy, helps with my business and always lets me choose where we eat. He esteems me as one of the most thoughtful, hard-working women he knows.

(Ok, fine, he also loses his temper sometimes, is a tiny bit too sensitive for my taste and has yet to figure out that a hamper is in fact designed for holding dirty clothes, rather the floor or the bed where they inevitably end up. But other than that, he is pretty great.)

This is Spring Break week, which means I have an extra list of things I'd like to get done. House projects and writing and extracurriculars for the kids, organizing and sorting and tending to the yard - all things that get put off until another day, a day when there's more time. Spring Break, to me, is *the more time*.

In preparation for our big week off, I gear up with my list and I sketch up hourly plans for how to best fit everything into the week (okay, fine, today was broken down into half hour segments). The Amazing Husband offers his support, adds a few of his own items to the list and we set out for one of the most productive Spring Breaks in human history. I am salivating as we walk away with lists in hand.

We have slotted in family fun time - head to the library one morning, go to the pool for a day - and in exchange, schedule several kiddo trade-offs to give each other a chance to check several more boxes off our to-do's in the productive luxury of kid-free space. The Amazing Husband gets up early all week to fit in the gym and grading and planning curriculum and then heads home mid-morning for family fun or to give me my turn out. I try to relax into the idea of a Spring *Break*, practice letting go of a few of the to-do's, attempt releasing my grip from some of the unnecessary musts. I fight my inclination to define every hour of our day by how much we have produced or accomplished.

Halfway through the week, I start to feel good, both about our progress in checking off to-do's, and in the amount of family time we are sharing. Midmorning rolls around and it's time for a kiddo trade-off. I'm gearing up to head to a coffee shop for a few hours of writing after playing hard with the kids since the early hours of the morning. The Amazing Husband, having woken up well before me, comes home and welcomes the kids with big hugs and huge smiles. He starts packing them up for a playdate with their cousins, but there's some chaos in the transition - shoes that cannot be found and socks that need putting on. Nothing out of the ordinary. Nothing I haven't calmly dealt with a dozen times before.

But, today, *I crack.*

Right in the midst of my husband's generosity and joy, I critique and scowl and fuss. I point the finger and blame him alone for all the chaos. For no conscious reason at all, I warp into Jerk of the Century and create a hell around us all. My thoughts flurry and fume: *He's taking too long getting their bag ready - why is he even packing sandwiches? I can't believe I got them dressed and he can't even put their socks on! Oh my God, why is he still standing there?!* It's almost an out-of-body experience, warping into the Jerk and becoming a total minefield of negativity. I am both completely aware and yet, somehow, completely unable to change course. I see myself spiraling and I wonder, *What the hell's wrong with me?! Why can't I see what a wonderful man he is right now? Why can't I just be thankful? Breathe, breathe...*I remind myself.

I see the kids, seeming oblivious to all the bickering, carefree as they put on shoes and socks, and I smile gently at them. I watch them squirm, help tie a shoe, button a jacket. I hug them goodbye, fearing that they are already used to the snapping, the tension, wondering if cracking and fuming is their norm. I find myself feeling guilty, hoping they do not see. I wave at the door, trying desperately to plaster on an *"everything's-wonderful-kids"* smile.

Oh, *that smile.*

The car pulls out of the driveway and almost as soon as they are out of sight, my anger turns inward. I am filled with self-loathing and shame. My judging finger reverses its fuming gaze and starts shaking blame and critique twice as hard at me. I reel in self-hate and ask myself for the hundredth time, maybe the thousandth, *How did I get so lucky?! How does he put up with me? Why do I snap so easily? Why am I so awful at loving? How long will he even stick around?*

I linger at the doorway and see a shocking image of what all of this - all of me - may look like through my children's eyes. I freeze at the realization, wary but aware. I see the performance: The arguing in the car and the smiles when we arrive. The distance at home and the laughing in public. The impossible standards and the toxic negativity. I am profoundly aware of all the forced *"everything's-wonderful-kids"* smiles plastered over frustration and anger and deep fear.

Oh, *that smile.*

In it, I see pieces of my childhood, and I realize in that split second that even at two and three, my children see it all, too. They are breathing it in, taking it in as normal, as the natural way of life. My mind fast forwards ten years down the road, twenty, and sees them, like me, *becoming* the performance. Hiding their feelings, plastering on smiles, refusing apologies and avoiding hard conversations. Then I see them *uncovering* the performance, despising and dissecting the double standard, fighting to un-become. I foresee their confusion and their struggle.

This momentary glimpse of *could be's* takes my breath away. My heart sinks further, my body finally bending at the weight of it all, finding rest on the doorstep. Even though I am aware that my self-loathing is dramatizing and exaggerating the images running through my head, I cannot help but see it all as a warning sign as well. I cannot help but be shaken and troubled, searching for answers, for help, for hope.

My mind moves slowly, trudging through a cloud of negativity. I feel depleted, emotionally empty from fighting with myself. There on the doorstep, I cannot come up with a coherent thought, until finally a word appears like a flash: *Unless. Unless. Unless...*

I finally pry myself off my concrete perch and head out to a local coffee shop. I am soon reminded of my last encounter with this word, *Unless*. The kids were snuggled in their fleece pajamas, their warm bodies like an intoxicating security blanket on my lap. We read Dr. Seuss's *The Lorax* and now I replay the storyline in my mind: After the

Onceler has exploited the land and the animals and his family for the sake of profit, he finds himself in a dark, polluted land, completely alone. All that remains is an ominous stone in the midst of decay and ruin. A stone with this inscription: Unless. It is a mandate to the Onceler. And in true wise-but-accessible Dr. Seuss fashion, he writes, *"Unless someone like you cares a whole awful lot, things are not going to change, they are not."*

Somehow those words seem to be exactly what I need to hear and I sense the initial echoing of *Unless* is divine. I step back from the fear, from the forecast of impending doom. I try to let go of the shame and let the echoing resume, sowing hope deep into my soul: *Unless, Unless, Unless.* Like the Lorax and his stone inscription, I cling to the possibility of something else, the mystery and beauty of what *could be.*

It is subtle and yet profound, the change that washes over me from this one little word. By the time I leave the coffee shop, the cloud of negativity and self-hate I was trudging through just hours earlier has cleared. In its place is a ray of possibility, a lightness, even joy. Not that the road ahead seems easy or even clear, but instead of bumps and fog, I see a road of possibility. I sense with the lifted clouds that I, too, can find a clearing and create change.

And I know I must. I must walk into something new. I will not live the performance. I cannot be loving mother and critical wife, tender nurturer and ungrateful nag. I cannot be Mama Dear and Jerk of the Century.

I cling to *Unless.*
I bend with apology.
I rise with hope.

~:~

In hindsight, I am always in love with my husband. I cannot say enough of his care and kindness, his faithfulness and hard work. Yet, sometimes, in his presence something warps, morphs, even freezes in place. It leaves me asking myself, *What am I trying to protect? Defend against? What am I hiding from?*

I know it is not him, but me. Perhaps, *I am scared.* Scared to be so thoroughly and deeply known. Scared to be out of control, to be rejected and vulnerably seen. Scared of being unwanted, unneeded, abandoned. Scared that all my deepest fears will be proven right, that the raw wounds will be scraped open again.

I'm tired, too. Exhausted. In my fatigue, I find it so much easier to live the pattern, to keep the performance going. I may hate it, but I know it. Plastering the *"everything's-wonderful-kids"* smile on feels like second-nature. I subconsciously snap at one, then hug another. I allow the false self, the Jerk of the Century, to control my responses to my husband, to be a bandage over my vulnerability, a perceived barrier between my heart and possible pain. But he deserves more and the kids deserve more. And I am coming to know that I, too, deserve more.

Marriage often feels like an uphill battle, deeply rewarding but incredibly taxing. So often I feel stuck, defined by all the barriers I've put up to protect myself, constricted by all the arguments and baggage, years and years of blame and disagreeing and picking out each other's weaknesses. So often I have felt hopeless, unchangeable, unable.

Today, *Unless* is capturing my heart and my imagination, and is reminding me, convincing me, all is possible. And in trying to flesh out what that means, to put breath and life into a word, I have had to ask, *Unless what? What change can I affect? How would my true self act? How would she love? What would she say and, even in failure, how would she go on?*

She would say thank you, speaking gratefulness often. She would keep it simple, but frequent. Thank you for working so hard today. Thank you for making me coffee every morning. Thank you for giving me time alone. She would count her blessings daily, knowing, voicing, that he is amongst the greatest of them all.

She would be free to touch tenderly, to hug, to kiss. She would let romance happen, not overthinking the past or the rules or the excuses. She would look into his eyes more. She would be present. She would accept his offerings with grace, esteem his effort as enough. She would let herself, and him, and today, be *enough*.

With gratitude as her morning alms, she would make apology and forgiveness her evening offering. She would say with sincerity, with conviction, *"I'm sorry."* She would own the mess, the judgments, the negativity. She would own them and she would forgive them and she would choose better. She would assume the best, of him and of herself, and move in compassion. She would name the good, speak the hindsight *now*. She would make laughter her song. She would push past the discomfort, the pricks of vulnerability and let her heart be held. She would press in when it is hard. She would not withhold; she would give and know and be known.

I know She is in there - that She is perhaps the truest me. There are days I feel almost wholly her, awake and connected to every step, every word, every decision. But there are so many other days - like the fuming, finger-pointing, smile-plastering days - that she is a distant shadow. She seems foreign and unattainable.

One of my favorite authors, Sue Monk Kidd, wrote in her book *When the Heart Waits*, this profound line: *"The art of soul making is taking our lives in our hands and - with all the love and discernment we can muster - gently whittling away the parts that don't resemble the True Self."* With the hope and courage of *Unless*, I stand, whittler in hand, choosing day-by-day to walk and whittle away on this journey of becoming Me, thankful to have my husband by my side.

Writing Prompt: Wrestle with the idea of *vulnerability* in your writing today - how are you showing up and letting your true self be seen to those closest to you? How are you shutting down and hiding behind masks of fear or anger or plastered happiness? How deep and real is the intimacy in your life?

RUNNING

*How limited the world would be if we confined ourselves
and God to what we think is impossible.*
Sue Monk Kidd, *Firstlight*

In eighth grade, I joined our middle school's track team. As far as I can remember, my motivations were based purely on social acceptance - what others thought of me, both socially and physically. I was well on my way down the road of body-loathing at the time, trying every fad diet, stolen diet pill and exercise regime I could get my hands on. Running at track practice for an hour or so a day seemed like a perfect step toward gaining the dream body I was always chasing after. I imagined long, lean legs, a flat stomach and narrow hips. If I won a race or two along the way, all the better.

I was also well aware of the social ladder one had to climb in most public schools. I wanted to be liked, accepted, admired, cool. Most of the kids that seemed to hold that status were involved in one or more sports, so I realized I, too, would need to sign up for a sport or two. I was totally uncoordinated with any ball-oriented sport, which narrowed my options significantly, leaving me with cheerleading, track and swimming. I chose to participate in all three.

I ran track that eighth grade year, and then again my freshman and sophomore years of high school, competing mostly in the 400 meter individual race and the 4x400 meter relay race. I was mediocre at best - never first, never last. I did at least do well enough my sophomore year to earn a Varsity letter in track. But, very soon after that, I made the Varsity cheerleading squads for both football and basketball seasons and decided to switch my attention exclusively to cheerleading in my Junior year.

Even though my track days were over, I continued to regularly run short distances for exercise over the next couple years, sometimes as much as five days a week. And yet, despite all those early years of running, I can never remember a time when I actually *liked* running. It was always a means to an end for me - namely, a better body and more friends.

Fortunately, the older I got, the more I allowed myself to have actual likes and dislikes, so that by the time I turned twenty I embraced my hatred of running and for all intents and purposes, swore never to run again. When, years later, I decided to give up on exercise altogether, I was thankful to think of running as exclusively in my past. *Or so I thought.*

A whole decade later, I found out I was pregnant with my daughter, Havyn, when my son, Kyler, was just over two months old. I was still healing and carrying extra weight from my first pregnancy, in addition to fighting extreme fatigue from a colicky newborn. I had no energy to fight the sleep deprivation or the cravings of this all-too-soon pregnancy, and as a result did my fair share of emotional eating. By the end of my second pregnancy, I was more than fifty pounds heavier than my healthiest weight.

I was fearful of going on a specific diet, afraid I would reignite the old dieting obsessions and self-hatred. I was also nervous to introduce too much exercise back into my life, in case it ended up making me more exhausted and even more ravenous for food. Although my body image had improved significantly since those teen fad-diet years, I had found that peace largely through abstinence. For the most part, I had never learned a truly healthy balance of nutrition and exercise. I was unsure how to reintroduce those things into my adult life now.

And so it was with hesitation that I decided to try to shed my post-pregnancy weight by training for a 5K. We registered as a family for a fun event that would take place the summer of 2012, a few months after Havyn's birth. To prepare, I began strictly following the "Couch Potato to 5K" training schedule, walking a lot at the beginning and slowly, *slowly* - over the course of twelve weeks - building up to a three mile run.

Race day came and went, and with the support of my youngest sister, I ran all 3.1 miles. I was proud to have run the entire race and thankful to have lost some weight throughout the process. I was also equally relieved that all the running was over, so that I could now resume normal living, active but never intentionally exercising. My tennis shoes found their usual home, securely stowed away in the back of my closet.

~:~

My tennis shoes peacefully rested, collecting dust in the back of my closet, for the next two years. Then, yet again, what once seemed to be a forever part of my past came lurching back into my present, this time with increased intensity and frequency. Thanks to my *"101 Things in 1001 Days"* list, I found myself training for a triathlon and a half marathon this past summer. I know, *Wait, what?!* Let me back up for a minute.

As I have shared before, my *"101 Things"* list has been a true blessing and a real joy, paving the way for many wonderful family memories and unique experiences. It has encouraged me to focus on what I value most and has pushed me to reach for goals I never really thought possible. At the top of the "absolutely impossible" goals list, was to compete in a triathlon and run a half marathon, both of which have been desires and dreams of mine for years. Very distant, daunting desires and dreams, at that.

After making my *"101 Things"* list, I found myself quickly skipping past those two physical goals, subconsciously willing them to disappear. I was terrified to actually commit to and train for either event. Finally, several months into my list hopscotching, I knew it was *"now or never."* That with my teacher-husband's summer schedule, and with the kids in a pretty manageable flow, this would be the summer to invest the time into training. This would be the summer to add a time stamp behind those goals.

And so, late this past Spring, I researched local races and found a sprint triathlon held in mid-July and a half marathon held at the end of August. I registered for both events, knowing that if I dished out the money, my frugality instinct would have a hard time not following through. I Googled "half marathon training schedule for beginners" and found a myriad of options, all of which overwhelmed me with their running distances and frequencies. I sat, jaw-dropped, at the thought of running five days a week with mileage totaling up to thirty or more miles a week. Maybe I didn't care that much about accomplishing this goal after all? I mean, really, *I do hate running.*

Finally, I chose the "Couch Potato to Half Marathon" training schedule, since it seemed to fit my fitness level best, and had worked for my 5K training two summers earlier. It started slow, lots of walking and running combos, interspersed with weight training and low intensity cardio. Somehow, within 15 short weeks, it promised to have me ready for thirteen miles – well over two hours of straight running! Never in my wildest dreams, nor in my worst nightmares, could I fathom running for over two hours without stopping.

The end goal was absolutely implausible to me, so I trusted in the training schedule and kept my eyes on one day at a time. I solicited the camaraderie of friends and family and found a few willing victims to start the training with me. We inaugurated our training with a two mile walk/run at the end of May. Distances stayed relatively manageable for the first few weeks and allowed me to build up some confidence in my ability to run. By the time our long weekend runs were up to six miles, I started to feel like a runner, albeit still unable to imagine more than doubling my longest run to the full thirteen mile goal.

I wheezed through side cramps and gave in to a new pair of nice running shoes, after nearly destroying my knees with my four-year-old pair of off-brand sneakers. True to his nature, my husband was fully supportive, making time for me to run, offering constant affirmation and even surprising me with a new road bike and gear.

I started to look forward to my weekly ride, felt my legs getting stronger and my lungs filling fuller. Although my runs remained a constant mental and physical challenge for me, they also offered me a place of mental space that I grew to love and relish. I found myself reciting reasons for gratitude with each breath and often ended my run filled with the joy birthed from thankfulness. Still physically excruciating, running became a mental and spiritual resting place that I grew to treasure.

My distances increased, my times improved, and before I knew it, mid-July rolled around and I found myself days away from my triathlon. I still had not managed to work in a chance to swim and although I had historically been most confident about the swimming leg of the race, I now started to worry that my total unpreparedness would put me under before I even got to the biking and running legs of the race. My fears seemed confirmed when two days before the race I attempted a short open-water swim and was winded within ten yards.

On July 17, well before dawn, I picked up my youngest sister, loaded our bikes into our minivan and headed for the beach where the race would be. We would be completing a quarter mile open water swim, followed by almost twelve miles of road biking and ending with an off-road two mile run. I was a ball of excitement and nervous-energy, triple checking every detail and playing the race over and over again through my mind. My husband came with the kids just moments before the race started, and there on the beach, in my speedo and swim cap, I was filled with a tremendous sense of gratefulness and privilege.

Some combination of race-day adrenaline, deep-seated thankfulness and two months of training hurled me through the swimming leg and kept me strong in the biking and running legs. I enjoyed every second of the event, felt strong and thankful for a body that allowed me to participate in this life-long goal and was already contemplating future triathlons by the end of the race. I finished first in my age bracket and 12th overall, and although the event only included 200 people, it was an achievement I was both proud of and couldn't stop marveling at. *Did I just do that?!*

My mind and body were accomplishing goals I never thought possible, leaving me to wonder what else I may be capable of, what else was just a couple months of determination away. When I got home, I wrote in bright red ink *"7/12/14!"* beside *"Compete in a Triathlon"* on my *"101 Things"* list.

~:~

Unfortunately, even with the mental high from my performance in the triathlon, I had a hard time the following week getting back into my half marathon training. My body was clearly fatigued from the race, right when my weekend runs were entering distances of 8, 9, 10 miles each. With the encouragement of my husband, I found myself at the end of a day's run, day after day. Eight miles, done. Four miles, done. Six miles, done. Three miles, done. *One mile, one run, one day at a time.*

I followed the training schedule and continued to push into the open mental space running offered. I told my mother-in-law, *"I'm not the kind of runner that just loves to run. To some degree, I dread it every time. When I'm running, I constantly oscillate between loving the open roads and hating myself for setting this goal. It's a battle to put one foot in front of the other every time I go out."*

Finally, two weeks before the half, I went out for my longest run yet: eleven miles. Still over two miles short of the race day goal, it was the longest distance I would complete before attempting the full 13.1. I struggled and ached my way through the final half of the run. I quit a quarter mile short of my training goal, and feeling defeated, wondered if I had hit my limit. An ache in my right knee and hip quickly turned into intense throbbing that kept me from walking normally for hours after my run. Even with days off and extra ibuprofen, my knee and hip pain continued to return, affecting me mentally more than anything. For the first time in weeks, I began to feel uncertain as to whether my body was capable of completing the half marathon at all.

I took my last two weeks of training very lightly, hoping that extra rest for my joints would help more than the detriment of missing those last several training miles. When race morning rolled around, I was physically and mentally excited, but hesitant. I wanted to stay within a nine-minute-mile pace for the race, a pace I had kept through most of the last month of training. If I kept that pace, I'd finish under two hours, which was a goal I had set my heart on weeks earlier.

I started the race very amped up and, in hindsight, over-confident about the pace I could maintain. I oscillated all the way from a 9:45 per mile split to an 8:15 per mile split - back and forth, back and forth, every half mile for the first four miles. I had a hard time finding a natural pace with so many other runners around and so much adrenaline pumping inside me. Once I finally realized that I was overdoing it and needed to relax into a steady pace, it seemed to be too late.

By mile six of the run, I felt my first wave of exhaustion and started to panic at how soon I seemed to be crashing. I tried and tried to get lost in my mind - listening to music, practicing gratitude, coaching myself along. I had my phone for pacing, using the same app I had used throughout training to hear my split pace every half mile. I managed to maintain my desired average pace all through mile nine, but was much more winded than usual and discouraged that all the race day adrenaline hadn't produced any extra speed or endurance in my running.

To add to the discouragement, every time my phone notified me of a new half-mile mark, the distances got further and further off from the official race markers. So, for instance, my phone announced I had hit three miles at least fifty yards before I passed the actual race sign marking mile three. At mile six, that distance had increased to a hundred yards, and so on. By the end of the race, my app clocked me in at 13.5 miles *before* I even hit the 13 mile marker. Needless to say, *that last half mile felt like an eternity!*

At mile ten, I was totally depleted. Physically and mentally exhausted, frustrated, discouraged. As much as I kept trying to remind myself that I could do this, that this was a once-in-a-lifetime opportunity, that I didn't want to have any regrets, *I truly had nothing left to give.* I was moments away from just stopping. Then, as I rounded a corner and saw mile marker ten, a woman about my age, cheering along the side, looked right into my eyes and with emotion said, *"Come on, you got this!"* I literally started bawling.

I choked on tears for the next few minutes, trying to catch my breath and will my legs to keep moving. As much as I did not want to stop, as desperate as I was to finish strong, it felt physically impossible to keep putting one foot in front of the other. By mile ten and a half, I was convinced that I needed to walk for a while. My pace dropped to ten minutes per mile.

Miles eleven and twelve are an absolute blur. I was in so much pain, so emotional, so mentally exhausted, so ready for it all to be over. I had stopped caring about a certain pace, I just wanted to get to the finish line as fast as I possibly could so that I could never, ever run again.

What felt like a million steps later, I *finally* crossed the finish line and blacked out into the first volunteer. After being helped back up, I wobbled my way to the sidelines to greet my family. I remember almost yelling, *"That sucked! It was awful! Worse than childbirth! I am never, ever doing that again!!"*

I was sick the next two days and very sore for most of the following week. I found out later that my official time was just *over* two hours - three minutes longer than my original goal. For a while, I wrestled with having fallen short of my desired time. I could not figure out what I had done wrong and the perfectionist in me needed a good excuse. I struggled to embrace the achievement with pride in light of my disappointing final time. I was so frustrated to have trained so hard, sacrificed so much, and to have come up *just* short.

That frustration momentarily morphed into insanity, causing me to seriously consider jumping right back into training for another half marathon that would be taking place later in the Fall. Thankfully, the reality of jobs and kids and normal life reconvening pushed my insanity into a state of dissatisfied acceptance. I practiced embracing my imperfections, checking off *"Complete a Half Marathon"* with genuine pride. My tennis shoes found a comfy spot back in the closet - not in the very back, but rather, resting up front, ready for anything.

Writing Prompt: Write about a time you worked hard to accomplish a goal or did something that had previously seemed impossible. Try to articulate what *impossible* means in your life.

COOKING CLUB

Storytelling has always been at the heart of being human because it serves some of our most basic needs: passing along our traditions, confessing failings, healing wounds, engendering hope, strengthening our sense of community.
Parker Palmer, *A Hidden Wholeness*

Some people say they have a *"green-thumb"* when it comes to gardening success. Or a *"way with words"* if they are a natural orator. Then there are those that have a *"real knack in the kitchen."* While I would never classify myself with any of these sayings, I have historically been especially inept in the culinary arts. In fact, this *lack-of-knack* in the kitchen lead a friend of mine, years ago, to challenge me to bake a loaf of bread. She suggested it as a spiritual exercise, a way to practice vulnerability, knowing it was about the furthest possible thing out of my comfort zone that she could possibly suggest.

I accepted the challenge and ended up baking that loaf of bread, feeling extremely awkward and self-conscious the entire time I did so. I meticulously followed the recipe, studying each step for at least five minutes before feeling confident enough to move ahead with measuring or mixing or - God-forbid - kneading. The final product was edible, mostly good, but I was emotionally exhausted and did not attempt any further culinary endeavors for several more years.

Then this past winter I read a lovely book by Shauna Niequist called, *Bread and Wine*. Niequist is a beautiful storyteller, and I soon was enthralled by the experiences she described, all relating to mealtimes. She captures the warmth and connection between food and relationships, how cooking for and with one another is such an intimate act. As someone who loves to host dinner parties and birthday celebrations, I was moved by the way she spoke of caring for others *through* her care for what she fed them. She spoke often of her conviction that we should be able to feed ourselves, and I was soon convinced, too.

Up until reading that book, our family ate slightly healthy, *extremely* simply meals. A standard dinner would be a pile of fettucini boiled from a box, with a spoonful of alfredo sauce heated up from a can, served beside a pile of frozen broccoli zapped in the microwave. If we were feeling a little fancy, or if there were guests, we would add a grilled chicken breast to top it all off.

For the first eight years of our marriage, our spice cabinet consisted of salt, pepper, garlic powder and chili pepper flakes, all of which were added at-will to *most* dishes we cooked. I never purchased a fresh herb or even fresh meat. We cycled through ten or so simple, standard meals, nothing ever even requiring a recipe (unless you count the box instructions for how to make a brownie mix, which was just about our only dessert option). Although I had taken tiny steps in the culinary world since having kids, we largely stuck to those ten staple meals over the years.

And so, you can see how profound a book like Niequist's was to me! With all her fancy talk of mincing and pureeing and roasting - I was totally out of my comfort zone, but totally inspired to be there. Motivated by a desire to create beautiful memories, including the delicious food that was served, I decided to commit to try at least one new recipe a week. I knew I needed to keep things simple even with the limitation of just one recipe a week, so I restricted myself to recipes with ten ingredients or less. I started a Pinterest board and aptly named it, *"Easy Cooking."* Although I was walking into the kitchen, I was going to do it one step at a time.

The very first recipe I tried was a chicken avocado salad - seven ingredients and five easy steps. My husband grilled the chicken, which is his speciality, then we cubed it and tossed it in with diced avocado, lime juice, cilantro and green onions. It was my first time squeezing a fresh lime, my first time mincing fresh cilantro and my first time whisking together a homemade dressing. *I loved it all.* The light mayo-lime dressing added just enough moisture to make the avocados slightly creamy. The flavors mixed together into a refreshing, delicious summer staple. I served the chicken salad on romaine lettuce leaves, and was thrilled with my successful first try.

During that first month of adventuring into the kitchen, I tried lots of new recipes, including homemade blueberry zucchini bread, a creamy cilantro lime dressing served over rice bowls, and zest-of-lime parmesan zucchini *(the bread we loved, the creamy dressy was okay and the parmesan zucchini we never tried again.)* I also gave some of the recipes from Niequist's book a try, including her sweet potato fries with siracha dipping sauce and her white chicken chili, both of which are now family staples. I added to our spice cabinet cumin, cinnamon, chili powder and dill. I bought a basil plant and nurtured it by the sink and we added cilantro and mint to our garden. Soon, I was starting to feel like I had a place in the kitchen after all, and my family was loving this new experiment.

As I continued to read Niequist's book, and my joy in cooking grew, the idea of a Cooking Club started to take root in my heart. Niequist writes about her own group, and what captured me most from her stories was not the cooking itself, but the sense of true community the members experienced through their monthly meeting. I soon found myself sending an email out to my closest friends with this enthusiastic appeal:

Hi friends! This is an invitation, because I SO thoroughly enjoy you. And a bit of a read, so feel free to come back after the kids are in bed if necessary!

I recently finished a book called Bread and Wine, a lovely memoir of a thirty-something living and loving and learning about life, often through food, or at least around the table with food. (It's a quick, enjoyable read if you're at all interested.) In one of her chapters, she writes about a group of friends that form a Cooking Club and end up experiencing deep loss and great joys together. She says this, "It seems like we've been meeting together forever, but we realized last night that it's been three years this month, and that's worth remembering for me - that it doesn't take a decade, and it doesn't take three times a week. Once a month, give or take, for three years, and what we've built is impressive - strong, complex, multifaceted. Like a curry or boeuf bourguignon, something you cook for hours and hours, allowing the flavors to develop over time, changing and deepening with each passing hour on heat. You don't always know what's going to come of it, but you put the time in anyway, and then, after a long, long time, you realize with great clarity why you put the time in: for this night, for these hours around the table, for the complexity and richness of flavors that are so lovely and unexpected you're still thinking about them the next day."

I love these words and cannot get past the first line about what can be built in small increments, with a little bit of effort. While our kids are young, while our schedules are packed, while our minds are weary - purposefully carving out time to be, to connect, to enjoy - so that hopefully down the road, when the next big storm hits or when we need a good laugh, the connections will be exponentially stronger and the memories will be full and satisfying.

I go on in the email to give some logistics, ideas about where to meet and when. I let them all know that I am not expecting a lifelong commitment, but am drawn to the idea that an intentional time just once a month could turn into something so meaningful and magical. I offer my home for the first gathering. Then I hit send to the eight most amazing women I know.

In less than an hour, the first friend responded with enthusiastic interest. By the end of the day, all the others had responded with equal excitement and interest in pursing the idea. We quickly agreed on meeting the last

Friday of each month, and started planning our first menu, which ended up being a hodgepodge of everyone's favorite recipes. One friend made baba ganoush, I made the beloved chicken avocado salad mentioned earlier, another friend made a quiche and others brought cookies and chocolate and wine. We cooked and ate and chatted through the evening.

The next month we went with a Mexican theme, and Beth hosted in her adorable, newly-wed apartment. She made the most delicious fish tacos topped with an amazing creamy dressing over cabbage slaw. One friend added homemade guacamole and I brought a fiesta bean salad, best eaten as a dip with tortilla chips. Of course we had margaritas, and sipped and dipped the night away around the coffee table, talking about life and kids and world health.

Our little group has continued to meet once a month for the past six months now. Once we did a *"Julie is Nesting"* gathering, and made homemade chickpea burgers for Julie to stock up in the freezer for when baby arrived. Another month we did a birthday celebration for two of the members and made, by request, fajita burgers and sweet potato fries. We've done a Thai-themed evening, with incredible peanut curry and scrumptious Tom Kha soup. And we always make sure to have plenty of dark chocolate and wine.

Just this past month we decided to include the hubbies and kids for a Fall Party. My family hosted, providing a make-your-own s'more bar with Ghirardelli chocolates and

Reese's and Nutella. The other families brought chili and cornbread and drinks. Some of the kids jumped in a huge straw pit we had created, chasing each other around the back yard and then wrestling in the straw when they returned. The less rambunctious kids enjoyed the sand table or the playhouse or ventured inside to find puzzles and toys. I spent much of the evening getting my baby fix with everyone else's littlest ones, marveling at the blessing of friendship I was surrounded with.

~:~

Several months after that original commitment, I am still trying new recipes in the kitchen, slowly but surely finding a place of belonging there. All this month we have been making batches of apple crisp and homemade granola and applesauce. My kids *love* cooking alongside me, and I am grateful that I found inspiration to step out in the culinary world in time for them to get to have these experiences. Together we are measuring and stirring and cooking, savoring smells and licks and the wonder of meaningful community, built *bit by bit.*

Writing Prompt: Write about a time in your life something greater came to be as a result of *"bit by bit."* Where could you use the hopeful principle of *"bit by bit"* in your life right now?

THE GREAT TRIANGLE

When the pilgrim journeys to a place beyond what he calls "home," his senses are heightened, his vulnerabilities are brought to the surface, and his perceptions are tested...he is able to be fully present in his journey amidst the discomfort and uncertainty, the mystery and the beauty.

Lacy Clark Ellman, *Pilgrim Principles*

My husband and I were both big travelers prior to having children. Having grown up with very little exposure to other cultures or opportunity to explore other nations, I caught the international traveling bug at age seventeen, while my husband's traveling days date back to his preteens. Combined, we have traveled to India, Thailand, Germany, Poland, Czech Republic, England, France, Italy, Spain, Guatemala, Honduras, Mexico, Canada and South Korea. I lived in Germany for a semester; he lived in Honduras for several months. Together, we lived in Thailand for almost two years.

We focused less traveling energy stateside, but still have accumulated our fair share of favorite U.S. destinations - the beaches and cityscapes of Chicago, the views and natural wonders of Sedona and our own family-friendly Columbus. We have summited Pike's Peak in Colorado, walked the boardwalk of Santa Monica beach in Los Angeles and camped along the Appalachian Trail in West Virginia.

Always, travel has meant to me adventure, new doors, new beginnings. I have loved the challenge of learning new languages and the intensity of exploring new cultures. While every overseas experience was not perfect, all introduced me to worlds unknown, both in myself and in the sights and souls surrounding me.

But like much of life, our traveling habits changed dramatically once we had children. In the past five years, I can count on one hand the number of times our little family ventured more than an hour from home. With the kids so young and the battle focused primarily on everyone getting as much sleep as possible, we have limited our overnights to Papa and Gilly's, just thirty minutes away. And even the amount of packing required for those simple stays is enough to fill a minivan and leave your head spinning.

It thus came as a surprise – *to myself and to my husband* - when this past Winter I spontaneously suggested that we embark on a 6,000 mile, 6 city, 13 day summer road trip. The trip would triangle us around to multiple families' and friends' homes, allowing us to check off several locations from our *"101 Things"* list, including *"Visit Atlanta & Stone Mountain," "Go to Texas,"* and *"Visit the Webster's."* I proposed the trip for the following summer, still several months away. With so much time to prepare and our *"101 Things"* list as tangible motivation, we soon agreed to give the trip a try.

Our trip would start at the end of July with a sixteen hour overnight drive to Lake Cypress, Texas. There, we would get to vacation with much of Daniel's family, including his

Gran and Gramps, whom the kids had only ever met briefly during infancy. From there we would scoot over to Dallas for a couple days, then head on to a day of sightseeing in New Orleans, a city Daniel had always dreamed of visiting. From New Orleans, we would follow the panhandle for twelve hours down to Sarasota, where we would stay with long-time friends. Finally, we would leave Florida and head back north, stopping in Atlanta for a couple days to visit my childhood stomping grounds.

~:~

By early Spring, we had booked hotels, reserved a rental van and finalized our travel dates. When departure day finally arrived, we had baskets filled to the brim with books and snacks for the kids, neatly organized bags of outfits and swimming gear stowed away in the trunk, and a recently gifted car DVD system from my husband's parents installed. The kids - at two and three - were excited, but mostly ignorant about the long drives ahead of us. We locked up the house, buckled up, *and then we were off!*

The overnight to Texas was even smoother than we could have expected. After watching a movie, the kids and I got a good night's sleep, while my husband conquered all sixteen hours of driving. Despite his lack of sleep, we all arrived joyful and refreshed, excitedly greeted by grandparents, aunts, uncles and cousins.

My husband's Aunt Paula and Uncle Darrell hosted us all in their beautiful lake house and Dallas home. The kids spent hours jumping off the dock and swimming in the lake. We got to take them on their first jet ski ride, watched daddy surf behind the "fast boat" and feasted on a traditional low country boil, the kids loving every messy minute of getting to eat corn and sausage and potatoes and shrimp straight off the table! We all ate well, played long and slept hard. It was as memorable and relaxing as any true vacation should be.

After such a successful overnighter heading to Texas, we mistakenly decided to adjust our travel plans, making the next leg of our journey an overnighter as well. Thus, around midnight on our fifth day of vacation, we left Dallas and began the eight hour drive to New Orleans. The kids slept fitfully, by which I mean, our daughter, Havyn, threw a demon-inspired fit for a solid two hours of the trip. Somehow, our son, Kyler, managed to more-or-less sleep through her antics, although the quality of his sleep was evident in his own fit-throwing the following day. Daniel's fatigue from a second overnighter, combined with my exasperation at Havyn's behavior and own lack of sleep, culminated in a hellish stew of mood swings and short tempers the following day.

We gave New Orleans our best shot, and although that is not saying much, we still left convinced that the city had very little to offer our family. Besides a delicious round of beignets at the acclaimed *Café du Monde* and a long awaited mule and carriage ride around French Quarter, we were underwhelmed, over-tired and ready for that leg of our trip to end. We all fell asleep by 9:00 that night, and despite the four of us sharing one king-sized bed, slept until 7:00 the next morning.

We packed and left New Orleans as quickly as we could, getting a head start on our twelve hour trip to Sarasota. It was a long day in the car, but the kids napped well and everyone seemed refreshed and much more pleasant now that we were out of the city. We watched lots of movies, ate way too many french fries and Twizzlers, and counted down the miles until our final exit.

After an entire day of southward Florida driving, we finally arrived in Sarasota and were warmly greeted by our hosts and one of their sons, Judah, who had managed to fight off sleep longer than all the other boys. We would be spending our three days in Florida with these dear friends, Chris and Terra Webster, and their four boys, who were once our neighbors while living in Thailand. Together, our families had shared some of the most unique, most memorable and also most painful memories of our lives.

Chris and Terra were by far our closest friends while living in Thailand. Living just across the street from us, we had shared meals together constantly - rich Tom Kha soup at the "Green Restaurant," delicious homemade carrot cake from the toaster oven, dozens of iced coffees and fresh rotis from street vendors, and late-night runs to the corner 7-Eleven for ice cream. We rode elephants beside each other, took motorcycle adventures up treacherous mountain paths together and navigated our way through Visa runs and immigration interviews. We watched each other's kids for date nights, vacationed together, worked together, laughed and cried together.

The Webster's know intimately a piece of our life journey like nobody else does, having been our only friends to witness firsthand our lives while parenting our foster son, Makham, during the six months we cared for him. They were the only ones to see us moments before and moments after the devastating loss of having him taken away. They also knew firsthand the struggle of life and ministry in Thai culture, having also experienced a painful betrayal in friendship and ministry while living there.

For these reasons and others, the Webster's had remained close friends of ours and we were thrilled to finally be making the trek to their Florida home. With six energetic kids, we stayed busy with trips to parks and fountains and our favorite: Siesta Key beach. The kids spent hours running in and out of the water, building sand castles and catching sand mites. Back at home, they dressed up like super-heroes, chased each other around the trampoline and when we finally made them sit still, the older ones read books to the littles. There were dozens of wardrobe changes a day and far fewer fights than we had anticipated. Again, we found ourselves experiencing vacation as it should be: *memorable and relaxing.*

We woke the kids and departed Sarasota at six in the morning on the first day of August. The kids went back to sleep for a couple hours, long enough to keep them from feeling too antsy during our eight hour drive to Stone Mountain. We had planned to stay in this Atlanta suburb for two days, revisiting all my childhood memories and enjoying the historic Stone Mountain park and downtown. But no sooner had we taken our exit, than did we realize that the quaint, beautiful little town of my childhood memories was no more.

Instead of a bustling main street, with craft stores and local cafes and gift shops, we found a deserted road, worn down buildings and the occasional beauty shop. We drove on, increasingly bewildered by how drastically the town had changed in the decade since I had lived there. Finally, finding nowhere to buy dinner, we headed back to our hotel, and I decided to go out alone the next morning to do one more round of exploring and reminiscing.

As I drove through Stone Mountain early the next morning, I was silently sobered by the changes of time. I drove past my old elementary school - that place where I first learned to achieve, to belong, to write - and saw a tiny, corroding brick rectangle with rows of trailers behind. I drove back down Main Street, taking side roads in hopes that we had missed some local treasure the night before, but found only chipped paint and empty buildings around every turn. Past the local library where I fell in love with *Cam Jansen* and *The Babysitter's Club*, where I first discovered my love for reading. Past the old Hardee's, where my mom had treated us kids to three-for-a-dollar hamburgers and a shared large fries, now a bare-bones Church's chicken shop.

Finally, I headed to our old neighborhood, where both lovely and haunting memories had filled my mind and heart for years. Past my old bus stop and the stewardess's home and the hill that I sped down and landed with a concussion. Past the home of my first crush, the high schooler that I had hand-delivered a love note to as an eight-year-old. Around the cul-de-sac where my best friend, Coventry, lived and where we had enjoyed dozens of neighborhood block parties together. Past the Perez's where we had Easter egg hunts, the Bello's whose backyard dock treated us to hours of wilderness pleasures. Down the hill to that half-constructed home whose empty halls had been our fort through several Georgia summers.

And then there was our home, that beige split level whose lawn was once so well-manicured, with a fence of red tips that my father doted on year-round. That lovely home that had been the backdrop of so many of my childhood memories: my sisters and I lined up in a row in our matching Easter dresses on the sidewalk, standing together in front of the fireplace on Christmas morning, birthday parties and sleepovers and watching my baby brother being born.

But now the red tips were gone, the grass was overgrown and the porch had been repainted white. Surreal swirls of long forgotten memories came rushing back, mixed with the bewilderment of so much neglect. I spent another hour slowly driving around, taking lots of pictures, quietly soaking in the old memories and the new sights.

Later that morning, we climbed Stone Mountain, Kyler proudly summiting all by himself. I continued to find sites that stirred up childhood memories, filled both with sorrow at the changes of time and joy at having been able to reconnect with all those pieces of myself. We spent that afternoon with my Uncle Mitch and Aunt Liz in their north-Atlanta home, then returned to Stone Mountain for our final night away.

We were all eager to get through the last leg of our drive and, after almost two weeks away, finally walk into our home again. The ten hours back north was smooth and uneventful, with nothing but corn fields and a traditional Cracker Barrel lunch to mark the time. As we neared home, Daniel and I started daydreaming about our next summer adventure. *Maybe this time we would head west, visit the Grand Canyons and camp along the way? Maybe we would repeat the same circuit, replacing New Orleans with a less tourist-driven coastal town? Or what about heading north, exploring the New England states which had remained mysteries through both of our traveling days? Boston, New York City, all the way up to Maine?*

After over seventy hours of car time and 6,000 miles added to the odometer, we pulled back into our driveway and started unloading the van. Home felt even more like home after having slept in so many different beds over the past two weeks. We unpacked the essentials, started a load of laundry, then all crashed into bed - *our beds.*

That night, surrounded by all things familiar, I dreamed of dock jumping and sand between my toes, mountain climbing and endless roads ahead, family laughter, food around the table and a summer of memories that I would cherish forever.

Writing Prompt: What does *home* mean to you? How have your experiences with travel or other cultures influenced that definition? Describe a recent trip, exploring how feelings of vulnerability, discomfort and increased presence were part of it.

LONGING

It dawns on my that I've never walked beside someone in deep pain. I've been more of a drive-by friend, the kind who reaches out once or twice and hopes the situation will be resolved quickly. I care. I cry. I pray. But I don't stick around long. I'm the type of friend you would want around for a broken ankle but not for chronic depression.
Anna Whiston-Donaldson, *Rare Bird*

I moved from a suburb of Atlanta to a small town in southeastern Ohio midway through my sixth grade year of middle school. I had already switched schools once that year, having been accepted into an urban magnet school a month after the Fall session in my hometown began. I can remember my first day at both new schools with clarity - each classroom a polar opposite from the other. The Atlanta magnet school with its lively group of inner city kids in a creative, if not sparkling, space, compared to the rural farm town with its brand new, white walls.

In Atlanta, we spent our afternoons in ballet classes and rhythm workshops and vocal lessons. I was the only Caucasian in my grade. Just a couple months later, we moved ten hours north to Ohio, where I soon took my first steps into Logan Hocking Middle School. There, I would meet my first farmer, experience my first fair, enjoy my first days off from school because of snowy country roads. I became the overwhelming majority, with only one or two students in each grade adding any sort of racial diversity to the district.

Once settled in Logan, I was outgoing and confident enough to find friendship without too much trouble. I was accepted into a group of friends, whom I later realized were the "cool kids," and soon started attending sleepovers and birthday parties. My Ohio sixth grade peers were boy-obsessed compared to the friends I had left in Atlanta. The expectation was to have a boyfriend, and it was not uncommon, even at that early age, to be having sex with him. While I resisted the sexuality of these relationships, I was soon caught up in the boy-chasing world.

Lunch period and bus rides were the dreaded parts of my day, as these were the moments when everyone was expected to showcase their relationships through hand-holding and long kisses goodbye. In the lunchroom, a boyfriend's and girlfriend's chairs would be squished together as closely beside each other as possible, allowing for as much bodily contact as possible. Hands would sneak under the table and enmesh in a sweaty, thirty minute hand-holding ritual. Then, boyfriends would wait for their girls, walk them to their bus, and a peck, if not a slip of something more, would be required, along with the standard, "*I love you's.*" It was all so foreign, so embarrassing, and in hindsight, so age-inappropriate.

As I entered my eighth grade year, I dated a different boy each month, thrilled with the chase but less interested in the day-to-day realities of actually being someone's girlfriend. That year carried with it some of the normal middle school drama, mostly lots of letters exchanged in the hallways, precisely folded white rectangles declaring who had a crush on whom and who was best friends with whom that week. As long as somebody signed her note to me with "*BFF*" and someone else signed it with "*Love*," all was right in my tiny, middle school world.

My confidence was high but shaky, the reality of a confidence built on *others'* perceptions of my worth and beauty. I would soon learn the hard way that such foundations end in a devastating, downward plummet when said *others'* perceptions change. All year, I focused most of my time and attention on hanging out with my peers. It was not uncommon for me to be gone from my house multiple days a week, at some sleepover or party or after-school activity. I ran track to spend more time with friends, drunk beer to spend more time with friends, slept in tents and on trampolines just to spend more time with friends. My peers were my world.

A couple weeks into summer break, I left for a rare weekend with my cousins in a neighboring town, about an hour away. This was before cell phones and text messaging and Facebook, before you could be in multiple places at once. I was away for three days, during which time one significant party took place that I missed. I have always played the story out in my mind that it was solely my absence from that party that triggered the awful chain of events that were soon to follow. But in reality, I never was given any sort of rationale. All I know is that I was a thirteen-year-old girl obsessed with social acceptance, dependent on others' good opinions of me, and the day had come for that all to come crashing down.

At that historic party, a rumor was started that I was a lesbian. This was in the late-90s, in a small, conservative town, and well, let's just say it was not said as a compliment. I returned home from my weekend trip, and as any peer-oriented teenager would do, started calling my friends to catch up on their weekend. I am not sure now who I spoke to first, but the rumor was soon revealed and the person on the other end of the line just as quickly declared her intention *not to be my friend* anymore. I can still vividly remember how bizarre that first call was - so strange and unbelievable that I did not initially think much of it. It seemed more like a practical joke or a single person's act of twisted middle school vengeance.

But after calling another friend, and then another and another - each call ending in the same stunned silence - the reality of what was happening started to sink in, like a terrible nightmare that I could not wake up from. I can still see my thirteen-year-old self in those next few moments, moving in slow motion, life as she knew it completely falling apart. I can remember how disorienting and traumatic each successive phone call became. And I can remember finally falling into a heap on my bedroom floor in broken sobs at the cruelty of my friends.

As if those initial phone calls had not been traumatic enough, I would soon learn the true weight of these *you're-a-lesbian-so-we-cannot-be-friends* declarations. Each person stayed true to his or her word - I did not have friends, but rather, found myself with hateful enemies. On multiple occasions rocks were thrown at our house with notes folded around them, and messages were written on our sidewalks, all declaring the grotesque nature of me, the accused lesbian. On the one occasion I remember walking by the city pool that summer, alone, of course, someone I had never met yelled out at me, *"Dyke!"* in a repetitive, mocking tone. I was beside myself with shame.

Even at the time I was baffled by the absurdity of how deeply and quickly the rumor had taken root, especially in light of my past year's history with boys. I had dated dozens of guys, unfortunately making out with most of them. There was no logical reasoning I could ever figure out for why the accusation was originally made, let alone for why it spread with such speed and certainty.

As though my broken heart needed more to bear, I soon came down with mononucleosis. The infection caused so much fatigue, on top of the emotional weariness I was already feeling, that I spent the next several weeks of my summer mostly isolated in my bedroom, and often sleeping. For a season it hurt too much to talk, which was just as well since I had very little to say. I was far too embarrassed by the bullying to ever speak to anyone in my family about everything that was happening, and out of friends to chat with for hours on the phone.

At some point in that dark mono-bullying season, I realized I would have to start high school soon. The thought absolutely terrified me. I became so depressed and anxious about my pending first day of high school that I began to contemplate suicide. I had done some minor self-mutilating with friends earlier that year, an initiation rite of sorts, but always as little as possible to still be accepted. Fearful of physical pain, but desperate to be through with all the emotional pain, I decided to take a cabinet full of pills one night. My hope was that the cocktail of medications would induce a slow, painless death while I slept.

No sooner had I swallowed the last pill and returned to my bed, than did I feel an overwhelming desire to live. I quickly began to panic, too ashamed to tell my family what I had just done, but also fearful of what the impending consequences might be. And then, for the first time in years, the Divine crossed my mind, like a flash of hopeful light. I began to pray, to ask for help in jumbled words and with uncertain faith. I remember instinctively vowing to offer my life in return for a "free pass" out of this suicide attempt. I spent the next few hours in a state of anguished, trembling prayer.

Later that night I did finally fall asleep, and awoke completely healthy the next morning. The cynic in me later wanted some sort of concrete medical report to verify whether the cocktail of medications I had taken would have actually killed me. But at the time, waking up at all seemed to be a miracle. And for a long time I held tightly to the Divine encounter I'd had that night, finally feeling a renewed reason to live.

~:~

In my memory, the *entire* summer after my eighth grade year is hazed over with this darkness of bullying and sickness and suicide attempts. But in reality, the timing of it all must not have taken much more than six or seven weeks, because soon I found myself spending time with news friends. One friend, Ashley, and her mother, welcomed me into their home, where I began spending a significant amount of my time. I remember spending all day watching *Brady Bunch* episodes, or seeing *Selena* for the millionth time, or packing up the van to head to the river for a weekend of tubing and skiing and nights by the campfire. They soon were a second family to me and my heart began to heal in their company.

As the day approached for our first day of high school, I still felt a significant amount of anxiety. I had not heard from or tried to contact any of my former friends, and was nervous about those initial confrontations, scared that the bullying would continue. But during my time with Ashley's family, I had begun regularly interacting with God and had found a sense of belonging and confidence as a result. I had attended a powerful Christian retreat focused on love and forgiveness, and left that weekend feeling valued, empowered and deeply loved.

And so, entering the hallways of Logan High School that first day of freshman year, I tried to keep my focus on forgiveness and love, rather than on fear or revenge. Nothing dramatic happened, and in fact, as far as I can remember, the rumor had all but died out completely. Ironically, many of the people that were most heavily involved in that summer of bullying, soon attended the same Christian retreat I had, and started their own journeys of love and forgiveness. Many of our lives became regularly and richly intertwined throughout our high school years, and some of them I can still call friends today.

~:~

That experience of betrayal in friendship and trauma from bullying, although it came and went with unusual frequency, left a deep arrow in my heart. The arrow pierced me with this message: *You are not befriend-able. You are not lovable.* Despite healed relationships, despite genuine forgiveness, despite years of maturing and growth, the wound from that arrow left me with a deep insecurity that, frankly, I battle to this day. In many ways, ever since that summer, I have struggled to feel fully loved and welcomed in a friendship, just as I am. And as I am seems to be an intensely loyal person with a bottomless pit craving for meaningful connection. Perhaps by design, the arrow struck me, all those years ago, in a tender place of deep longing, a place akin to my truest self.

Although I test more on the introverted end of the spectrum, an ideal week for me includes multiple play dates, hosting dinner twice, and an evening out one-on-one with a friend. I love hosting parties and celebrations for any and every reason, and thrive on hours of soul-connecting conversation. For six of our nine years of marriage, Daniel and I have had at least one housemate, often two - siblings, friends and exchange students - packed into any spare bedroom we have to offer. Perhaps it is a gift of hospitality. Perhaps a desire to fill the longings for love. Either way, there is a passion for welcoming and loving and nurturing others, especially in our home, deeply embedded in me.

Yet as I have grown in the role of host and carer, I have wrestled with not feeling hosted or cared for myself. I have had some wonderful friends over the years, but more often than not, I have acted as the initiator, the planner, the one to call or follow-up or do the extra special thing. And I have felt wounded a million times over for calls that friends never made *to me*, for birthdays that friends never celebrated *for me*, for effort and love and kindness that seemed to be withheld *from me*. I have felt like *the unwanted, the unworthy, the un-pursued* at some point in nearly every friendship I can recall.

I spent much of high school and all of college leading Bible studies and small groups, mentoring multiple girls at a time. As a leader, my insecurities in friendship were amplified, because it was *my role* to be the giver, the initiator, the one pursuing. And I struggled regularly with the fact that my desire to be the one mentored was repeatedly unmet or denied. So, I fought and fought the message that I was not befriend-able, not worth pursuing, despite my daily experiences. I often tried playing the devil's advocate, questioning if my expectations were wrong, wondering if it was even realistic to want the sort of friendships I did. I admonished myself to continue sacrificing, to continue serving and giving, regardless of my own longings.

Then, when we returned home from all of our devastating losses in Thailand - with no ministry, no future dreams, no home, no son - I found myself for the first time in my adult life, completely unable to be the giver. Unable to be the pursuer or the initiator. Deeply needing someone to nurture and welcome and pursue me without receiving anything in return. And though some tried with more effort than others, I soon found that painful arrow embedding itself deeper than ever before, screaming its haunting message to me: *You are not loved. You are not pursued.*

Indeed, it was devastating to experience many of the relationships we had built through church and ministry crumble when it was us who needed cared for. We had so longed to return to the family-like community we had left, needing more than anything a place of rest and healing for our souls, but soon found that when we were not playing our casted roles, we were not welcome. We soon found ourselves isolated, socially on the outskirts, struggling to find new friendships as we entered our parenting years.

It took us two years to attempt entering a new spiritual community. With wounds and wariness, but with deep desire, we started attending a small group recommended by a family member. There were natural struggles to get to know the other members, but also a constant battle with the old insecurities. After a month of attending and not being pursued in anyway outside of the group meeting, I was ready to quit. And yet, and yet...and yet I so longed to be connected to others. I so believed in sharing all of life with others. And so, despite a strong inner battle willing me not to, I laid myself bare and became the initiator again. I reached out in vulnerability and started planning play dates and dinner dates and hoped that, in time, things would even out.

But through the entire year that we attended the group, the friendships were slow to grow, slow to gain any sort of momentum, and left me battling the old arrows daily.

There was rarely initiation from others, even after we opened up and spoke of our past experiences and wounds. At one point, it was explicitly said to us that the primary purpose of the group was not friendship, but that those needs were being met for others elsewhere. While the comment was intended to emphasize the "spiritual" nature of the group - their focus on reading the Bible and relating to God - it spoke to me of the un-befriended, unloved, un-pursued. When it came time for the group to dissemble, all but one friendship (which was originally formed outside of the group) immediately dissembled as well.

~:~

Time and again, the arrow has struck, stab, stab, stabbing its message. A friend does not call or initiate for a few weeks and suddenly that old message pierces me deeply and I am back in my bedroom as a thirteen-year-old, wounded and asking myself, *"Why won't she pursue me? What did I do wrong? Will I ever have a friend that pursues me equally as passionately as I pursue her? Will I ever feel fully loved?"*

As I write all of this, I realize it would be easy to get the sense that I am often depressed, lonely, sad. But the truth is, I am not any of those things. I am largely a very happy, very engaged, very secure person. I have some wonderful, healthy friendships and spend time with these people often. I am deeply grateful for all the people I can call *friend*.

It's just that the arrow lodged its message deep, years and years ago. And the tragedy of the arrow is that it is rooted in both deception *and truth*. It is rooted in the reality of real wrongs and actual betrayals, the true neglect of a missed birthday or an unengaged friend, the very real heartache of dismissed needs and of unmet longings. And then the arrow amplifies and agitates each reality, until the message is an all-out attack on the core of *me*.

For years, I felt guilty that I was not able to squelch the insecurities through my relationship with God. I heard the message over and over again that my longings were ultimately for the Divine, not for relationships with others. I judged myself with that message, berating myself that I could not even get a relationship with the Great Pursuer right. In all those years, I often allowed the religious message that "God should be my all," deflate and defeat my genuine need to connect with others.

And while today I recognize the very real longing to connect with the Divine and to experience healing, I could not agree more with Glennon Doyle Melton when she writes, *"Some people of faith swear that their God-shaped hole was filled when they found God, or Jesus, or mediation, or whatever else. I believe them, but that's not been my experience. My experience has been that even with God, life is hard. It's hard just because it's hard being holey. We have to live with that. If there's a silver lining to the hole, here it is: the unfillable, God-sized hole is what brings people together...Holes are good for making friends, and friends are the best fillers I've found yet. Maybe because other people are the closest we get to God on this side."*

Today, I acknowledge my desire to be loved and pursued, not just by God, but in flesh and blood by *real friends*. I walk forward in the belief that it is equally as spiritual to spend an evening in soul-to-soul conversation as it is to spend an evening in "prayer," for both are offerings to our Creator. I own the yearning within me to be connected, often and deeply, with others in my life. And so I fight the arrows and reach out, again and again and again.

Writing Prompt: What kind of friendship have you experienced in your daily life, and in your darkest moments? What kind of friendship have you offered? How has the human longing for love and belong worked itself out in your life?

IN TIME

Most people weren't looking for a faith that provided all the answers; they were looking for one in which they were free to ask questions.
Rachel Held Evans, *Faith Unraveled*

When I run, I begin giving myself a mental pep-talk around the half-mile mark. I almost immediately feel winded, achey, *ready to stop*. I am aware of a tightening in my neck and shoulders, feel the impact on my knees and ankles of each stride, and vainly attempt to make things a little easier, reciting over and over to myself like some sort of Yoga master, *"Lighter, softer, stronger."* I get side stitches and struggle to control my breathing. I tell myself to relax, to find a steady stride, to just keep moving. I self-coach, sometimes incessantly, throughout every mile of my run.

If I'm lucky, something catches my eye and distracts my mind from all the self-talk. For a moment here and a moment there, I lose consciousness of my body, of my pain and fatigue and the need to will myself along, and instead am taken by the sights around me, the simplicity and complexity of each element. I am aware of the beauty and mortality of everything.

I look up and see a gorgeous, sprawling birch, bright white and green against a clear blue sky. I look down and see a gentle brook, glistening in the sun as if on fire, radiant in its simple flow. I look over and see a large bridge, cars zipping by like flashes of lightning. Over there, an old fence and children playing. Up, a heron soaring, long, thin legs stretched and sturdy.

I am lifted, if just for a second, from the physical act of running into a place of deep gratitude and growing awe. My soul stands at attention to the majesty all around me and I am lifted into a true place of praise - a place, honestly, that I have not stood in for a long, long time. The self-coaching is paused and instead I pant prayers of gratitude with each stride:

Thank you, Divine Creator, for the blues and the greens and the browns.
Thank you for the glistening of the stream and this soft breeze on my cheek.
Thank you for the elegance of the heron and the majesty of the birch.
Thank you for trails and health and a body to experience all of it in.
Thank you, dear God, for breath and for life.

As I continue to run, these two contrasting truths become increasingly amplified in me: *I am deeply powerful and I am unquestionably mortal.* I begin to recognize a deep inner strength every time I complete another mile, every time I conquer a new PR. Despite the aches and the effort, I start to feel strong and alive and in control of my own course. Conquering one foot in front of the other, I feel capable of achieving anything.

And yet, too, in the midst of this growing sense of inner power, dwelling as a complete equal, I sense my own fragility. As I breathe in, breathe out, breathe in, breathe out, I am confronted with the reality that I am merely a breath away from no more. I notice a holy fear rising in me, a reckoning of the truth that I am the created. In light of the trees, the waters, the makings of modern man, I realize *just how small I am*. I see a cardinal laid to rest by the side of the trail, a mole crushed alongside the road, and I know such mortality of the flesh will be my end as well.

Running, I find myself marveling at how these contrasting truths, seem to so naturally coexist. How the sight of sun rays beaming through the forest canopy can bring me both to my knees in awe and to my feet in strength. How the sparkle of the brook can cause me to utter my first direct words of worship in years, and also cause me to embrace further my individual creativity and power.

I am Warrior, strong and able and ready to fight my battle.
I am Human, afflicted and frail and at the mercies of the gods.
I decide my course - my choices have power and influence.
I am responder, a tiny part in a holy tale.
I am divine, the icon of God.
I am mortal flesh, and to dust I shall return.

The weight of each truth sinks in with my every step; left foot: *strong*, right foot: *frail*, left foot: *divine*, right foot: *mortal*, left foot: *beauty*, right foot: *decay*. And I realize that it is the fullness of each truth that I have run from for so long - the realities of both my own beauty and power and goodness, as well as the truth of my own mortality and frailty.

I have long waded in the middle, denying either identity. I have believed that my essence is evil, inherently in need of saving, of changing. I have believed that I am not enough - not good enough, not strong enough, not faithful enough, not skinny enough or beautiful enough, not disciplined enough or worthy enough. I have let *not enough* suffocate the true goodness in me, turning the divine seed of my deepest self black and blue in the face, parched and paralyzed, blinded by a thick cloud of self-hate.

In the midst of such soul-mutilation, I have reached for clarity, for an external *enough* to lift me out of my pit. I have clung to religious answers that promise to make me better, stronger, fuller, immortal. I have listened to teaching after teaching, taking notes and applying to do's vigorously, constricting my life to meet all the standards, conforming myself to fit into all the boxes, sickeningly aware that I am *still* not enough. Hopeful that in clinging to these steps, to these answers, to this God, I can journey toward enough. Denying my own mortality by embracing a promise of eternal life, a clearly defined image of who's in and who's out and how it all goes down.

And so I have walked the *"narrow way,"* careful that I wouldn't be one of the ones to go down. But when death and loss shattered my neat images, I eventually woke up to the religious numbing I had isolated myself within. I woke up to the reality of mystery. I woke up, too, to the reality of my true essence, the reality that we are each seeds - sons and daughters - of the Divine.

~:~

A famous monk named Maximos, who resides on the ancient Mount Athos in Greece, describes three levels of spiritual maturity, as recorded by author Kyracio Markides in his book, *Inner River.* First, Maximos talks about the "slave of God," the person who relates to the Divine as *"a fearful overlord who can toss them into Hell if they misbehave."* I have heard pastors and teachers appeal to this person hundreds of times, with diagrams of the path to hell and descriptions of what to do and say to stay out of hell. It was, in fact, this very image of the Divine that first started me on my spiritual journey, with promises of eternal bliss in exchange for a specific prayer.

Next, Maximos describes the "employees of God," people who *"do good because they expect to be rewarded by God. They work to earn their place in Paradise."* This certainly describes the majority of my years within the church: an underlying belief that if I do X and Y, I am promised Z; that if I believe A and B, I am guaranteed C. Even with the "relational emphasis" of many modern evangelical churches, I was taught a constant connection between my rule-abiding actions and the outcome of my eternal destiny, between my religious beliefs and behaviors and the reward or punishment I would receive from God.

Finally, Maximos talks about the "lover of God." He describes this as a person *"who has come to know the true nature of God in His total and unconditional love for all people and all creation. They view all human beings as icons of God..."* I cannot help but feel this description of the Divine is worlds apart from the God I grew up believing in. That God, although "personal and loving," required certain prayers and beliefs and behaviors before you were considered part of the family. That God seemed equally concerned about whether we were attending the right meetings at the right church of the right religion, whether we were *really* putting all those teachings into practice, as he did about welcoming us with open arms. That God was known to a science, clearly defined and stated on paper, sign by the X if you want a seat in heaven.

I can recall sitting through teaching after teaching, with bullet points and 1,2,3's, on how to grow my relationship with God - an *individual* relationship that we were all supposed to be experiencing in very *defined, common* ways. And all because we had prayed a very certain prayer at some point that allowed us access to these divine truths. I never heard voices like Rob Bell's, who said, *"The Christian faith is mysterious at its core. It is about things and beings that ultimately can't be put into words. Language fails. And if we do definitively put God into words, we have at that very moment made God something God is not."* No, God was a list of beliefs on our church website, a book with precise answers to every human question.

~:~

Sometimes all the legalism of those early faith days seems startlingly obvious to me now. And yet, it is so much messier than that. There are personal perspectives and childhood experiences to sift through, genuine encounters with the Divine, all muddled and mixed with the rules and the formulas and the simple answers. Some days it seems like enough to say that there was just a lot of imbalance, that lesser things were emphasized over the best, that it has all just been part of the maturing process. *No harm intended.*

Some days I can say that God was in the midst of it all. Other days, the foul taste that my former fundamentalist-faith leaves in my mouth will not allow me to settle for anything less than a good, hard spit. And so I have spit, *sometimes with way too much force.* I have asked the hard questions and searched for new language and tried to find balance and truth in knowing the Divine. I have returned as a seeker and a skeptic, not aiming to please or appease, but to discuss and learn. When strict formulas are pushed back at me, when severe language of who is right and what is acceptable are put before me, I do not swallow them like the people-pleaser I used to be. I try to stand and listen for love, for humility, for beauty and goodness.

In doing so, I believe I am finding truth in unexpected places, like author Markides, who wrote:

> *"You can find lovers of God in all religions, just as you can find slaves and employees. In my opinion, anyone who cares to study the world's religions without prejudice or bias will realize that Christian saints and mystics have more in common with the sages of Tibet and India than with Christian fundamentalists."*

Maybe Markides and others are on to something. I will be the first to admit that there is so much I do not know. Every time I run, I am reminded that - despite my strength, despite my freewill, despite the divine seed that grows within me, I am limited. I am frail and error-prone. I am mortal, flesh and bones.

But in running, I have been taught, too, that I am part of the beauty and majesty I see all around me - the very crown of creation. I am spirit and goodness. And increasingly I find myself broken open, embracing this journey toward wholeness and truth. Today, in running and in writing and in life, I stand firmly on this: *that we are each a divine seed of God, that unconditional love is the root of* **all** *truth, and that much is mystery.* The rest will come in time.

Writing Prompt: In what ways have you experienced the three categories of spiritual maturity described by Maximos? How do you deal with the truth of your own mortality? How do you honor the divine seed of all humanity?

Noelle is a writer and a seeker, threading together her story of wholeness, connection, and freedom one word at a time. Noelle is a stay-at-home mama, a small business owner and a firm believer in human goodness. She writes regularly at nbrynn.com, where she encourages others to pursue the healing power of storytelling in their own lives. She regularly contributes to popular blogs, including An Inch of Gray and All Things With Purpose, and has been featured in articles at The Phoenix Soul and A Sacred Journey. She lives with her husband in Columbus, Ohio with their two children, Kyler (4) and Havyn (3).

ACKNOWLEDGEMENTS

Three years ago, I would never have believed that just over a thousand days later, I would be sitting with a completed book in hand, a book in which I had penned every word. I was too frozen from grief, too numbed by busyness, too unable to see past surviving each day. But there were those that did believe, those that saw past my pain and my fear and my focus on all the to-do's, those that believed *in me* and offered me a path of hope through their love and belief. To each and everyone of them, I send my sincerest thanks and my deepest love.

To Daniel, my biggest encourager and my best friend - thank you for seeing me through all of life's messes and for believing in something bigger still. Thank you for believing in *us*. To Kyler, who gave me the gift of motherhood again, and who gives me endless moments of laughter and joy daily. To Havyn, the greatest surprise of my life, whose beauty inside and out astounds me always. To Joel Makham, the son I first loved, whose smile still melts my heart. To Camryn, the son I wait for with great longing still.

To Crystal, for letting the bigger picture come full-circle, for evenings of wine and freedom, for a friendship beyond rules. To Whitney, for honest words and open hearts and endless cups of coffee. To Casey and Mandy and Rachel and Julie, for your friendship and encouragement throughout

4

the writing process. To Derek & Lori, for the gift of knowing you and your son. To the Webster family, who will forever be a part of our story. To the Cooking Club gals, who have become everything I had hoped for and more. To all the Judays, who I am honored to call family. To my mother, for the gift of life, and to Nachelle, for your continued friendship.

To Anna and Lacy and Amanda, for giving me the opportunity to share my writing and for contributing your own strength and stories to this piece. To Holly, for your editing help. To all the authors quoted in this book, especially Rob Bell, Rachel Held Evans and Glennon Doyle Melton, whose stories told me I wasn't alone, whose voices opened my heart to new worlds.

And to Loryn, who will always be in my heart, reminding me to love and live well *today.*

Made in the USA
Charleston, SC
23 August 2015